STONEHENGE SARSEN CIRCLE
Present Day

With the Flinders-Petrie numbering system of 1880

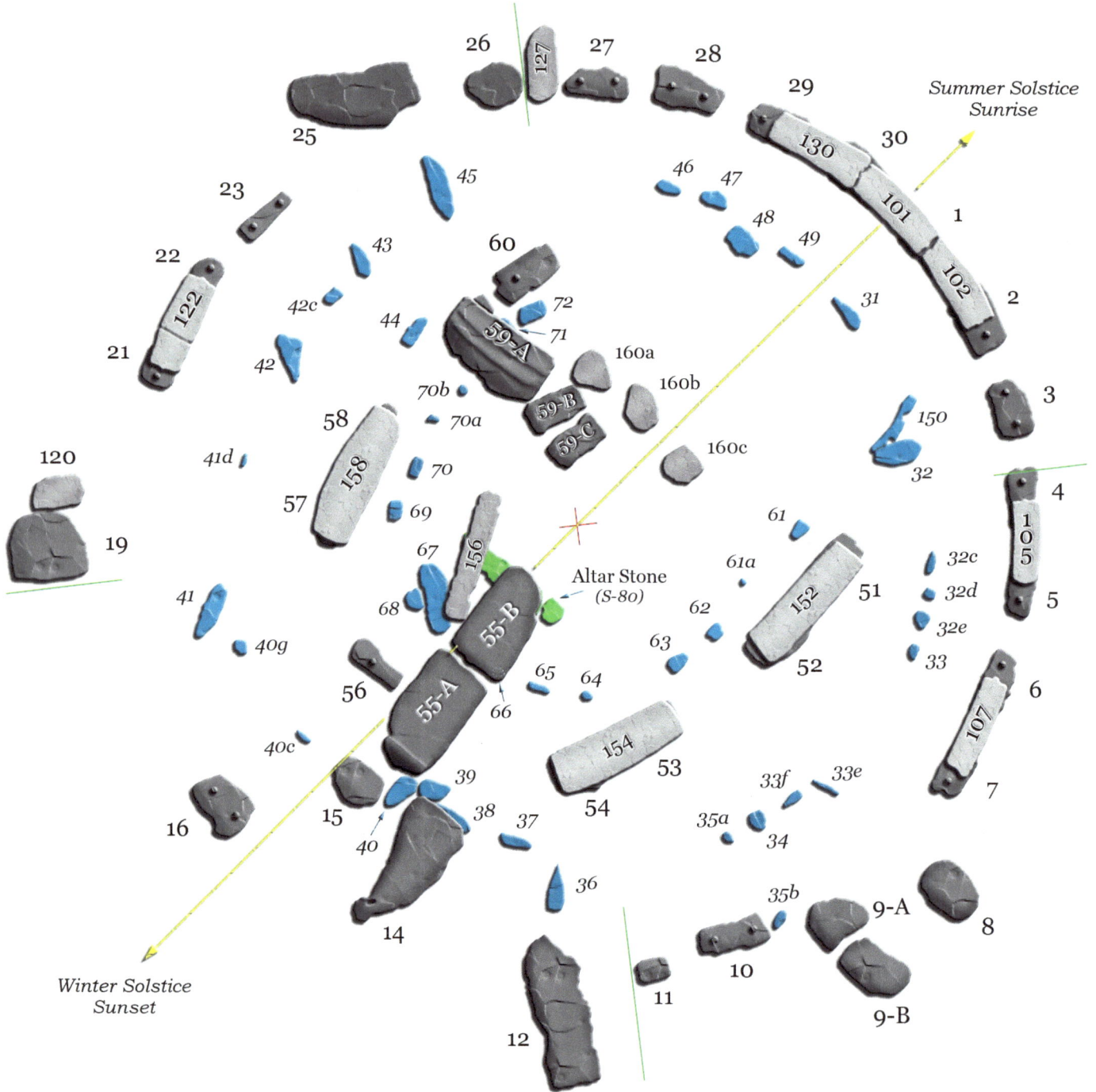

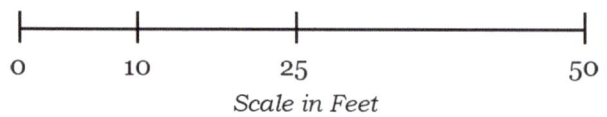

Summer Solstice
Sunrise

Winter Solstice
Sunset

Altar Stone
(S-80)

Sarsen

Lintel

Bluestone

0   10   25   50

Scale in Feet

STONEHENGE
and the Neolithic Cosmos

A New Look at the Oldest Mystery in the World

ND Wiseman

THE VINLAND PRESS

Cape Cod Massachusetts, USA

Stonehenge and the Neolithic Cosmos
is the sole work of its author. Any and all factual errors are his.

———————◆———————

In attempting to figure out what Stonehenge means I quickly
realized that no book of this type can write itself, while
this one in particular was an angry dragon on several levels.
Saying this, it would have been impossible without
generous contributions from the following people.

Simon Banton
Andy Burnham
Simon Charlesworth
Dr Rosamond Cleal
Sue Craig
George Currie
Andrew Davies
Dr David Dawson
Tim Daw
Peter Dunn
Brian Edwards
Pete Glastonbury
Aynslie Hanna
Dr Robert Ixer
Dr David Jacques
Mike & Dan Johnston
Austin Kinsley
Dr Terence Meaden
Jonathan Morris
Dr Mike Parker Pearson
Mike Pitts
Dan Rendell
Julian Richards
Adam Stanford

———————◆———————

For DORIS JEAN *and* NICHOLAS DEWITT

© 2018 by ND Wiseman All Rights Reserved.

NDWiseman1@gmail.com

ISBN: 978-0-692-36282-2

The Vinland Press, Cape Cod Massachusetts, USA.

Printing History: 10 9 8 7 6 5 4 3 2 1 *Revised Edition*

STONEHENGE
and the Neolithic Cosmos

A New Look at the Oldest Mystery in the World

ND Wiseman

THE VINLAND PRESS

Cape Cod Massachusetts, USA

Stonehenge c. 2000 years before present

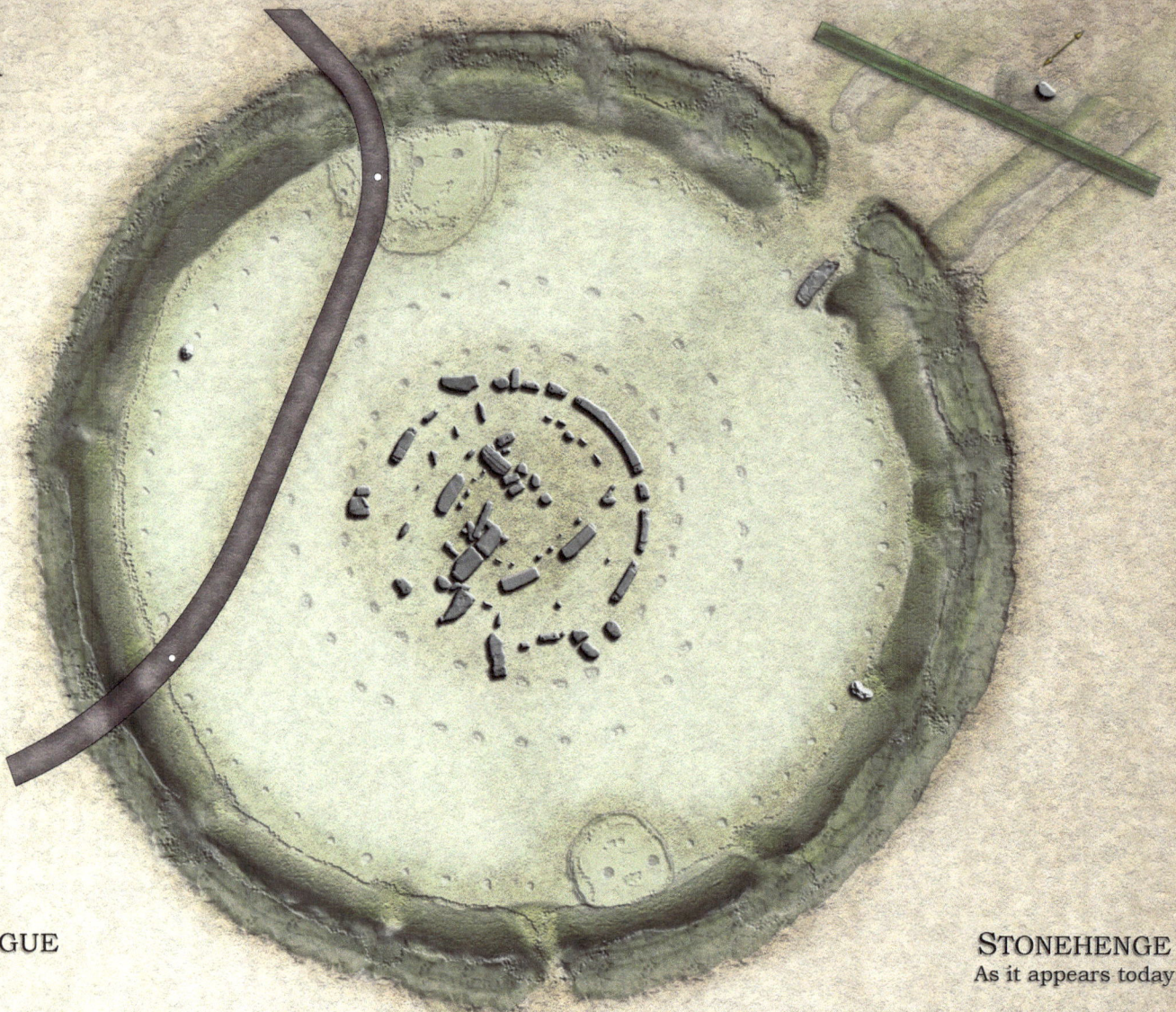

PROLOGUE

The deeps of fifty-one centuries have taken their toll on this venerable edifice and the cumulative vagaries of wind, water, ice and even earthquake have not been kind. But by the hand of man has the ancient complex suffered its worst disgrace. Forty percent of the stones are gone, leaving this bleached and crumbled death mask locked by time into the frozen rictus of ragged, gap-toothed ruin. Indications are that even the Romans played a role in its mutilation long ago. Robbed or slighted by pragmatism or piety for a dozen centuries thereafter, many of the stones have been smashed to rubble and carted off for mundane purposes now lost to the ages.

For more than five hundred years prior to the 20th century the site was privately owned, during which time the stones were relentlessly hammered at for souvenirs by gawking antiquarians, even as the ignorant sought King Arthur's treasure. While destroying wide tracts of archaeology, one pit was directly responsible for the collapse of the entire West Trilithon, which came shivering down en masse in early 1797. An apocryphal story tells of a local cottage industry which rented chisels to day-trippers, who would over time carve more than three hundred names on every surface; some known to history, most immortalized only by the hoary old greywethers.

The ditch and bank, cut across time and again with shepherd's trails, byways, or roads, are so damaged that they are only irregular dips and humps when seen from ground level. The tourist walkway, itself the remnant of one such track, has obliterated the North Barrow, while the South Barrow is little more than an outline in the turf.

Since 1918 Stonehenge has been owned and managed by the British government, during which time two major renovation projects have conducted repairs to arrest the degradation of this UNESCO World Heritage site. After years of legislative attempts, a section of the A344 road has been removed, so for the first time in centuries the Heelstone stands alone and the Avenue is unobstructed. 1968s cobbled ticket office has been closed and replaced with a museum-quality, environmentally sympathetic Visitors Center a mile to the west, thus returning Stonehenge to a more isolated landscape, with a partial restoration of its perilously compromised dignity.

What *is* Stonehenge, who built it and how long ago?

Some say that in the birth-pang of beauty, in a distant age before our race was born, the mighty stone henge sprang in whole part from the womb of the living world to become the remedial edifice which symbolized man's quest to harness the resonant electromagnetics required to commune with Gaia, the blesséd Earth goddess.

Or maybe it's just a weird pile of rocks dumped in the middle of nowhere a hundred years ago or something.

Seriously — who *really* built it?

Sinister aliens from beyond the stars visited primitive humans, found skulking behind nearby shrubs, and erected the mysterious moon stones using element-116 anti-gravity technology.   Then the experiments began...

Or perhaps the most ludicrous explanation of all: it originated some fifty-one centuries ago as the Citadel of the Cosmos, having been developed by a clever, knowledgeable and ancient people for the purpose of monitoring Sister Moon in her role as Keeper of the Dead. As over eighty generations passed, Father Sun and Mother Earth were introduced as the eternal life-bringers, wherein all three then ultimately defined and demonstrated the entire known universe itself, with those not-so-primitive humans rightly nestled in the bosom of all creation.

I know, I know — what goofy think-tank cooked up that *wacky idea?*

―――――――――――――――――――――●―――――――――――――――――――――

Among the most mysterious, iconic, instantly recognizable structures in the world, Stonehenge has for many centuries been viewed through a thick shroud of stark majesty; this shambling folly in grand decay, singularly stoic and alone out on the blustery Salisbury Plain, England. But a true understanding of its significance has been stymied within such poetic context. Only recently have certain objective, relentlessly prosaic observations inevitability incorporated themselves, and indeed the entire landscape, into a much larger perspective.

While Stonehenge is by far the most prominent feature in the area, it's hardly the oldest. It comes toward the end of a long line of Neolithic stone and earthen monuments found throughout the UK and illustrates a wide array of regional concepts which must have been thoroughly understood from time immemorial. But locally it's merely one element in a four-dimensional arena which includes Durrington Walls, Woodhenge, Bluestonehenge, the Cursus and the River Avon. Nearby, the vastly old, so-called Car Park Totems channel the later plains Indians of North America, although these enormous posts may never be fully understood. Coneybury Henge, Robin Hood's Ball and several long barrows are only a few among those on the list of precedents.

A mile or so east of Stonehenge, at the north end of a thickly wooded area known as Vespasian's Camp, is a site that was in continuous use from Mesolithic times well into the Bronze Age. At a warm spring called Blick Mead is found an old stopover for hunters and flint knappers which eventually morphed into a settled trading venue. It's swiftly becoming clear this long-lived encampment played a significant role in the area's development.

The Greater Cursus, only a few hundred yards to the north of Stonehenge, is older than the Egyptian Pyramids, and though it's been recognized for nearly three hundred years, nothing is known of its purpose. This narrow, parallel, dual-ditch earthwork is a mile and three quarters long and is sometimes described as a ceremonial partition between the worlds of the living and the dead. The most complete of several found elsewhere in England, *Cursus* means *Hippodrome* in Latin — a sporting arena — named so as it was, in the 17th century, assumed to have been built by the Romans for chariot competitions. Aligned more or less to the equinoxes, excavation has unearthed red deer antler tools used in its construction which date to 5,500 years ago — easily 3,000 years before any Romans existed and certainly 1,000 before Stonehenge had its pile of rocks installed.

Two miles northeast of the stones is found Durrington Walls, the largest henge in the UK, and it dates to about 5,000 years. So big it went unrecognized until the 1840s, foundations under its bank indicate that a community existed there prior to digging its huge ditch. A line of perhaps ninety postholes have recently been detected beneath the southern bank and these infer significant prior use. Excavation has revealed a town within where in a later incarnation, generations of devotees lived, worked and feasted at times of both solstices. People traveled to this place every season for 300 years. This is where the builders of Stonehenge lived.

Only 250 feet south of Durrington Walls is Woodhenge, so named because the six concentric rings of various-sized holes within once held stout wooden posts, perhaps supporting a roof. Yet another mysterious structure, the causeway in its embankment aligns with summer solstice sunrise — the same as Stonehenge.

There are many other features in the vicinity which help define the purpose of Stonehenge, and over the course of this book we shall explore a few, in hopes that this age-old enigma might be more completely understood.

Now, before we start, let me quickly say that this book does not 'Blow the Lid Off' other theories, or 'Reveal the Secret of the Stones!' I *do* have a few new things to say, it's true, but I don't think anyone's going to be gnawing their hand because they didn't think of them first. So relax – there's no sleepless nights in your future.

Except for maybe about that pesky murder, but we'll get to that by and by.

Like any tale the beginning can be put anywhere, but this one is complicated, so to avoid saying: 'Like they did back then …' over again, some backstory should be given. As mentioned, Stonehenge didn't spring up out of nowhere, and as unique as it is, still has precedent. These should be understood so the context makes sense.

The people of the Neolithic were the same as we are. There's been no difference physiologically or intellectually for two hundred thousand years more or less, so there's no knuckle draggers in our story. To understand them, turn off all the lights, TV, cellphone, tablet or laptop. No Twitter, Netflix, Facebook or Instagram. With none of these frivolous distractions, go outside, build a campfire and look *up* – at a much more interesting show.

Do this for a year.

You'll soon find yourself thinking like people did 9,000 years ago. Watch the seasons. Why is it cold in winter; hot in summer? Look for patterns. See where the sun rises, sets, and how it spirals incrementally up and down both horizons every 6 months. Why do the stars wheel around a single point in the sky as if suspended from a pole? Notice any cycles. How is it the night sky rolls a bit further west each night, revealing its entire dome over the year? Why does every movable object travel through those 12 star-pictures, while the ever-phasing moon wanders around with a mind of its own? Most importantly: why does everything up there appear to orbit *us?* With fits, starts and many mistakes, it'll take you and your descendants 1,000 years to get all this figured out.

When you believe these things to be completely understood, you may begin building Stonehenge.

About 12,000 years ago there was still a lot of water locked into the polar caps as this was not long after the last ice age. Because a now-submerged landmass, called Doggerland, connected Europe and England, the people who lived at the time could stroll between the two. Some of the mainland folk moved across and set up shop. Settling in the north, east and southeast of future Albion, they eventually fanned out in all directions, filling the interior vacancies. By about 8,000 years ago, the water had returned and Britain became an island.

With a name based on where their pottery was discovered, the Peterborough people who came began creating peculiar circular earthworks, and while some seem to be associated with an afterlife, they may have served other purposes too. On the way from London to Wales there's a low round hill that has three concentric rings dug into it at different levels. The upper ring encircles the crest and is the faintest, while the lowest is deep and has its spoil piled toward the top. It's been heavily plowed since the Middle Ages but enough remains to note a resemblance to similar features found in France, suggesting the idea had traveled with the people from there.

These structures are called *Causewayed Enclosures* by virtue of narrow terminals across the ditch sections. There's various styles, but this one, called Windmill Hill, is 5,700 years old and is among the first of its kind to appear. The following long-lived culture of the wider region have been assigned their name from it.

The Windmill Hill people soon began burying their high-status dead in *Long Barrows:* rock chambers covered with chalk and earth. There are scores of these communal tombs scattered all over the countryside, though only a handful are found to be especially situated or aligned with anything celestial. Among the oldest and most famous is the West Kennet Long Barrow. It's found three-odd miles south/southeast of Windmill Hill.

Due southeast of Windmill Hill an enormous circular trench was dug with its spoil piled high on the outside. This type of earthwork is called a *Henge* and appear to have been introduced to the Orkney Islands long before. Known as Avebury, it's the grandest of all the nearly 900 circles found in the UK. From the ditch bottom to the bank top was 65 feet in places. Four causeways interrupt the circumference and each had stonerow avenues leading away, while inside were two carefully positioned stone circles. Within these, a number of significant celestial events – solar, lunar and perhaps even stellar – could have been, and most likely were, observed.

South of Avebury, in sight of the WKLB, is Silbury Hill. Rising 130 feet, the flattened summit commands broad overlooks. Big deal – there are hills all over the place. True. The difference is that this one was made by humans and is among the most massive in the world. Taking a century, it was built with chalk rubble scoured from its frequently flooded basin. There are many theories, but no one really knows what its intended purpose was.

These and other projects were deeply entwined within the Avebury Complex for a thousand years.

The English county of Wiltshire is home to some of the most famous prehistoric structures in the world. A feature of Wiltshire, indeed much of southern England and parts of France, is that the surface is composed of limestone, or chalk. This bed was laid down hundreds of millions of years ago when Europe was beneath the ocean. Uncounted trillions of microscopic shells rained down from the surface for eons, and today, the White Cliffs of Dover are a dramatic example of this process.

The submerged land mass broke up as it rose and large volumes of sand swirled into the contours, settling on the chalk. This silicate bonded to create the dense layer of stone we now call sarsen. The land flexed, cracking this carapace, and by the time England found itself in the present configuration, the stone had shattered into the bits we see today.

North and south of the county are divided by a low area known as the Pewsey Vale. Above this, the hills contain great fields of stone, while within the Vale itself there doesn't appear to be any. This is because it's an old glacial outwash and silting covers most of the sarsen to a depth of twenty feet. It's there — you just can't see it. South of the Vale sarsen is in short supply because land contours and natural outwashing prevented the sand from establishing itself. There's exceptions, but a great deal more sarsen exists above the Vale than below. At Avebury, the people took advantage of the stones' proximity when building their monuments, while at Stonehenge, south across the Vale, it had to be imported.

In secondary studies efforts have been made to identify the track used to transport the stone, and several observations have determined the most likely route. It's shown as a dotted yellow line. A waystation appears to be situated at Marden Henge. Rivaled in size only by Durrington Walls, this site was relegated to footnote status for years and had homes and other structures built on sections of its bank, destroying it. I believe this was originally a stopover for those who did the hauling. An ancient ford has been detected across the upper Avon and seems to have been used for crossing the stones to the south. The route continues through the easiest geography until it reaches the long-known work station slightly to the north of the Stonehenge site.

Without formal use of a traditional wheel, the methods used to move these colossal blocks remain something of a mystery. Ongoing professional and amateur demonstrations have attempted to show the means by which this could have been achieved. Some methods are overly complicated, but many employ sledges lashed to the stone, which is then moved on log rollers. Complex algorithms are used to compute man-hours, distance and the numbers of people for support, but for some reason few of these data include assistance from livestock.

A peculiarity occurs when we notice that few of the hundreds of stones used at Avebury and the surrounding area are dressed, while virtually every one at Stonehenge is. Proximity to the source fields persuades us that it should be the other way around, and this seems to emphasizes the importance of the southern site.

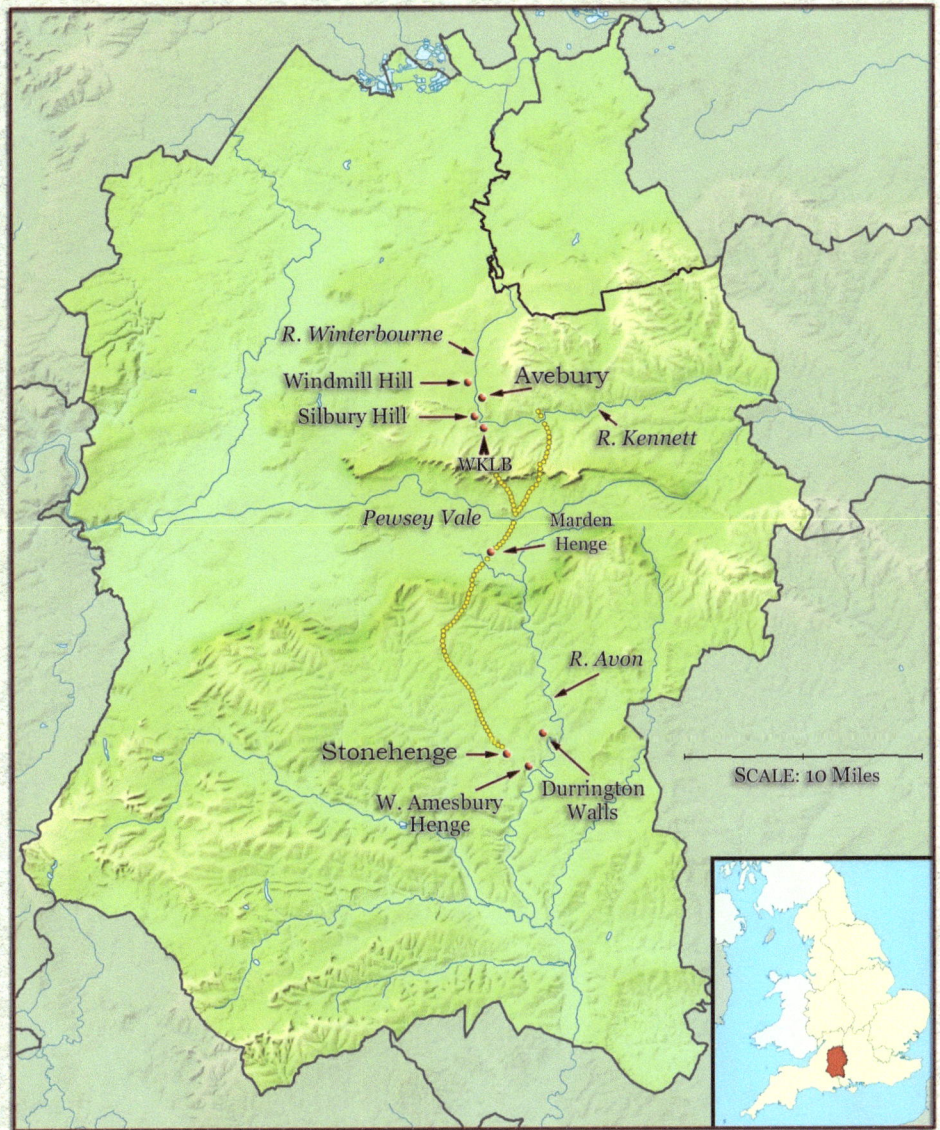

3

A few among many HENGES, BARROWS *and* STONE CIRCLES in the United Kingdom and Ireland.

Windmill Hill: *Causewayed Enclosure.*

Woodhenge: *Solar oriented posted henge.*

The Ring of Brodgar: *Large causewayed henge and stone circle.*

Devil's Den: *Cromlech, or exposed grave.*

Cursus Barrow Group: *Communal graves.*

Drombeg: *Small solar and shadow oriented stone circle.*

The Bush Barrow: *Single grave within a large cluster.*

Castlerigg Stone Circle: *Possible meeting place.*

Stonehenge: *Reverse causewayed enclosure with four discrete, solar oriented, shaped stone arrangements.*

Avebury's perimeter originally boasted between 98 and 106 stones. There were also two inner stone circles which were aligned to movements of the sun, moon and some say stars. The North Circle had a 3-stone Cove in its center, while the South had a 22-foot tall Obelisk. In total there were 215 stones at the complex. In the 14th century many were buried or broken up for building material, but in the 1930s Alexander Keillor, a wealthy marmalade magnate, dug up a large number and restored them to their original stoneholes. Work was abandoned due to the onset of World War II so quite a few remain buried to the present day.

Avebury Henge has had a village inside it for at least 800 years, and some say longer. It was the centerpiece within whose sphere a vast array of Neolithic projects flourished. About two centuries older than Stonehenge, its silted ditch was originally 30-feet deep and the embankment was once 35-feet high. Though smaller than the woeful remains of Durrington or Marden, complete articulation makes it the largest henge in the world.

The south perimeter stones average 12-feet in height.

One of two remaining Cove Stones.

5

Silbury Hill is the single largest human-made mound in Europe, and at 130 feet, is the tallest in the world. Forty-six hundred years old, composed of chalk rubble scoured from its basin, it was built in three stages over a century. Completed about the time the sarsens were raised at Stonehenge, its purpose is a mystery. Tunneled into several times since 1776, it has slumped in places and become quite delicate. Despite its robust size, visitors are firmly discouraged from scaling the now-fragile slopes. Sadly, the many advisories are often ignored and a number of rain-eroded trails to the summit have become permanent.

By design or coincidence, the Hill's slope mimics the angle of the rising moon's arc into the sky.

The Barrow is nestled in active farmland.

Added later, Blocking Stones sealed the Barrow.

This famous long barrow was built 5,400 years ago, but the interior remained largely intact until excavated in the 1950s. Centuries older than both Avebury or Stonehenge, it's 300 feet long, though only 45 were used inside. Situated at the crest of a hill, it overlooks Silbury Hill and other Neolithic sites. There's five chambers within it: two on each side of the central corridor and a large one at the rear. Aligned to Equinox sunrise, blocking stones at the front court were added later, sealing it.

Originally intended as a segregated communal tomb, the barrow was repurposed many times over its active life. Reconditioned in 2015, it's popular with visitors and has evolved into something of a mystical hotspot for trendy New Age hipsters.

The rear chamber.

The corridor in.

This is the Stonehenge Cursus from the west northwest at an altitude of 1,100 feet. It's a mile and three-quarters in length and has a long barrow outside the eastern end. Seen here is the reconstructed west terminal embankment, done in 1987.

Roughly aligned to the equinoxes, according to dates given by antler tools found in the ditches, it's 5,500 years old, though nobody has a real clue what it was for. One idea is that it acted as a kind of barrier between the lands of the living and the dead. The external bank might be a key to unlocking this age old mystery.

The trenches are three or so feet deep, with the spoil used to create the banks. The width of the earthwork narrows toward each end, but averages around 300 feet.

Centuries of plowing have badly disturbed it and further softened the ground view, but a late-day August sun brings out the contours.

It points directly to Woodhenge, unseen here, beyond the far end. At center are the Cursus Barrows, relatively recent neighbors to the structure. The upper right edge of the picture shows Stonehenge itself — dwarfed by both distance and comparison.

Below is shown the eastern terminal which was excavated in 2007. It hints in small detail at the volume of work required to complete these trenches, no doubt taking decades. Although the Cursus is 500 years older than Stonehenge, both ditch systems have sloped sides and a flat bottom.

The recovered tine of a red deer antler. Tools much like this were employed as picks to pry out lumps of chalk from ditch systems in the area. The shoulder blades of auroch were used as shovels. Workers often left their worn tools on the floor of the trenches.

Winter
Solstice
Sunrise

NORTH

This southeast aerial shows the remains of Durrington Walls, by volume at least, the largest henge in the United Kingdom. It's now so degraded the view must be assisted by a flattering outline.

Woodhenge is in the lower left, and though it's 200 feet across, appears modest by comparison.

The site was used as a settlement long before its enormous henge was dug, whereby Durrington eventually developed into a kind of Neolithic city for the people who came to build Stonehenge.

The red discs show the North and South Circles, discovered in 1967 when the modern road was cut.

Though posted circles are not uncommon, these consisted of huge oak timbers instead of the more usual pine, so they must have been imported, as none of such considerable size grew in this area at the time. Then, as workers continued the heavy lifting at Stonehenge two miles away, the folks here acted in a support capacity.

Comfortable, if spartan, homes existed for as many as 2,000 people, and for perhaps 300 years they traveled from every corner of the British Isles to participate in the labor and celebrations held here. Excavation analysis shows that during this period activity sharply declined at nearby Blick Mead in Vespasian's Camp, which is the oldest known, continuously occupied hunting and trading venue in the country. This suggests its eclipse by Durrington Walls for a time.

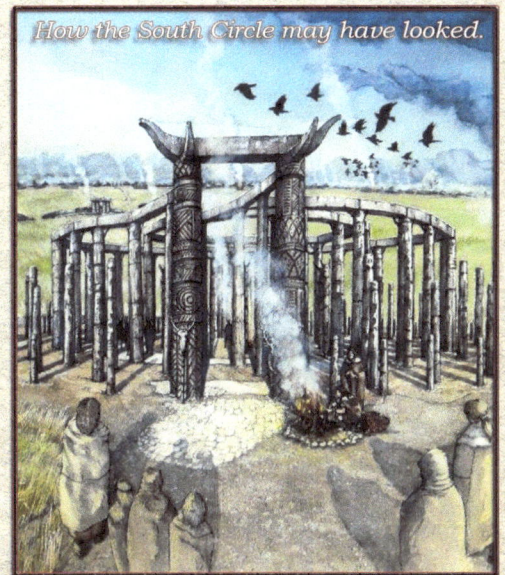

How the South Circle may have looked.

Each home has a waste dump, or midden, and each is filled with pig, deer and wild boar remains. Tooth maturity indicates the domestic animals were killed at nine months old, while the strontium isotope process reveals that many had come all the way from distant Scotland. In pottery shards the chemistry for wine, mead and beer is detected; clear indications of robust, communal festivities at both solstices.

A short, flint-paved Avenue to the nearby river Avon aligns with winter solstice sunrise, the reverse of Stonehenge. This sightline bisects the Southern Circle before passing through the opposing causeway exit.

Archaeologist Mike Parker Pearson kneels at the hearth of a Neolithic home excavated in 2008. Knee indentations in the chalk speak poignant volumes about the generations of families who tended this fireplace forty-five centuries ago.

THE STONEHENGE LANDSCAPE
Circa 1,600 BCE

N

1 Mile

The Lesser Cursus

New Visitor Center

Monarch of the Plain

Winterbourne Stokes Barrow Group

A 303

Cursus Barrows

The Great Cursus

Byway 12

Bush Barrow

A-10 *Disc Barrow*

Stonehenge

A-11 *Bell Barrow*

Normanton Down Barrow Group

New King Barrows

Old King Barrows

Coneybury Henge

The Avenue

Vespasian's Camp

Blick Mead

"Bluestonehenge"

River Avon

Amesbury

Woodhenge

Durrington Walls

Avon

STONEHENGE
Intact Appearance

Stone lintels not shown for clarity.

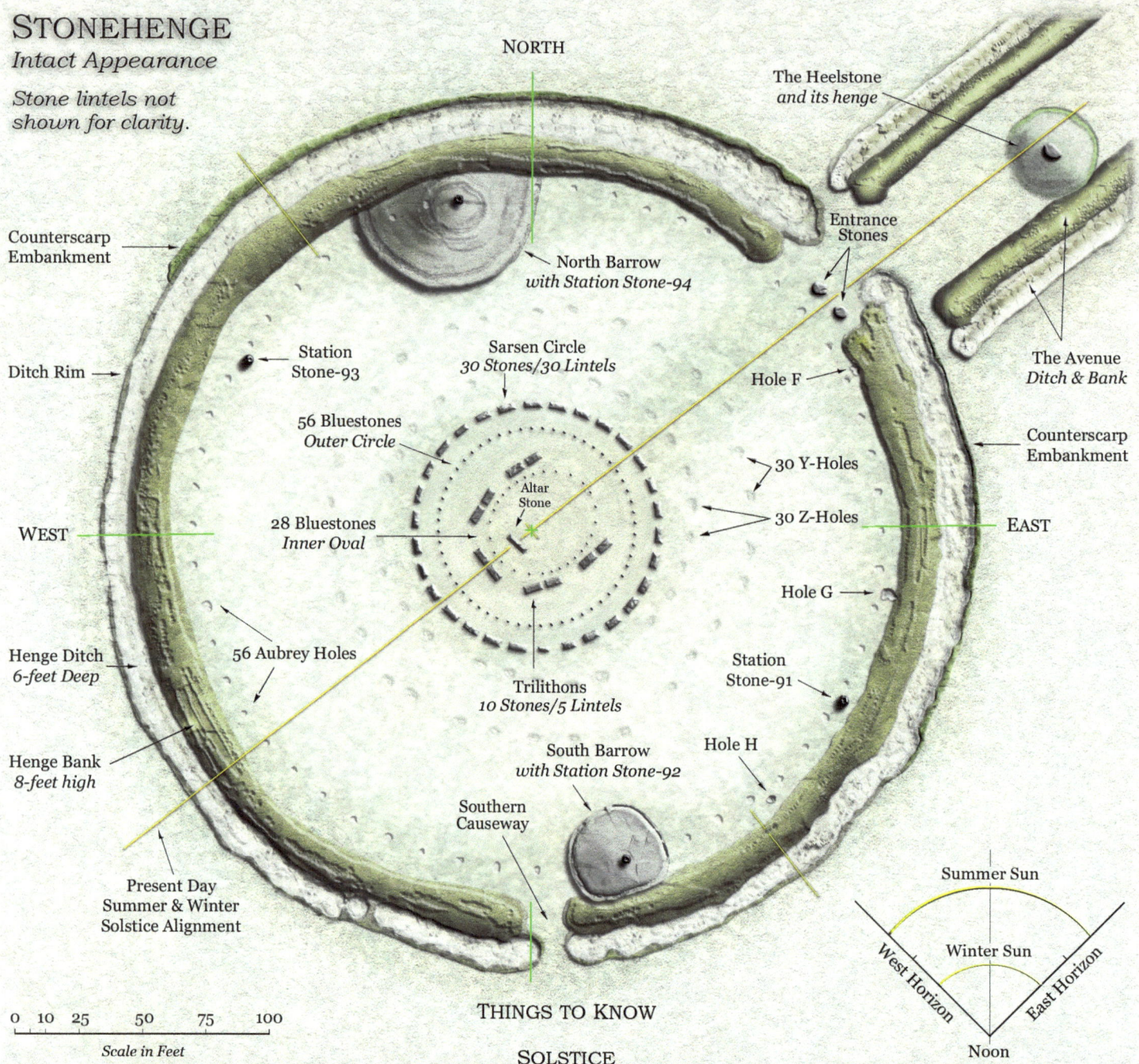

NORTH

The Heelstone *and its henge*

Counterscarp Embankment

North Barrow *with Station Stone-94*

Entrance Stones

Hole F

The Avenue *Ditch & Bank*

Counterscarp Embankment

Station Stone-93

Sarsen Circle *30 Stones/30 Lintels*

Ditch Rim

56 Bluestones *Outer Circle*

Altar Stone

30 Y-Holes

30 Z-Holes

EAST

WEST

28 Bluestones *Inner Oval*

Hole G

Henge Ditch *6-feet Deep*

56 Aubrey Holes

Station Stone-91

Trilithons *10 Stones/5 Lintels*

Hole H

Henge Bank *8-feet high*

South Barrow *with Station Stone-92*

Southern Causeway

Present Day Summer & Winter Solstice Alignment

Summer Sun

Winter Sun

West Horizon

East Horizon

Noon

| 0 | 10 | 25 | 50 | 75 | 100 |

Scale in Feet

THINGS TO KNOW

SOLSTICE

Twice a year the sun reaches its highest or lowest point on either horizon. In the northern hemisphere, 21 June marks the longest day because the sun arcs high overhead from the northeast. On 21 December, daylight is in short supply because the sun rises low from the southeast. The process is reversed for the southern hemisphere, where winter begins in June. All this occurs because Earth's axis is tipped to the plane of its orbit, and over the course of a year the sun's rays strike the surface at different angles. These points in time and space are relatively constant, changing only slowly over many centuries.

Because Earth is a globe, summer sunrise and winter sunset occur in opposition, or 180° apart. The ancient people were not only aware of this, but also of the pause in the cycle at either end, where the sun appears to stop moving for three days before beginning its northward journey once again. Traditions associated with this solar spiral have evolved over time, and because the sun directly interacts with all aspects of the environment — and is the key to life itself — it has influenced every culture in history, including our own.

EQUINOX

The mid-point of the sun's travel as it moves along the horizon; meaning day and night are equal in length. This also occurs twice a year, in March and September, and marks the beginning of Spring and Autumn — seasons which have their own associated traditions. With solstice and equinox, the year is neatly quartered by the sun.

Stonehenge looked much like this 3,600 years ago, though several of its elements were already incredibly old. For example, the ditch and Aubrey Holes were as distant in time to them as Charlemagne is to us. Below is a chronology of its major components.

———————————————————•———————————————————

NORTH BARROW: A pre-existing feature which was cleverly incorporated into the main structure. A double-ditched mound, its older, original purpose is a mystery.

HEELSTONE: A conical, undressed sarsen, this massive, interestingly shaped stone may have been laying on the chalk since it was formed. Known as Stone-97 in a previous incarnation, it is set within a small, single-ditch henge. Offset to the solar axis, its west side marks sunrise at summer solstice as seen from the henge center.

DITCH and BANK: Six feet deep and eight feet high respectively, the ditch was scoured out of the chalk; its contents heaped along side. With sloped walls and a flat floor, there's a wide causeway, or opening, at the northeast and a smaller one in the south. A number of the antler picks and shoulder-blade shovels used to dig it were left at various points on the ditch's floor. Unlike most other circles in the UK, the bank is on the *inside*.

AUBREY HOLES: First called X-Holes in the 1920s, these 56 pits were eventually named for John Aubrey, the 17th century antiquarian who may have discovered them. Though of irregular depth, breadth and spacing, they form a precise circle inside the bank. Originally cremation reliquaries, these holes held wooden marking posts, followed closely by bluestone pillars. Their use as an ingenious lunar calendar is currently being investigated.

ALTAR STONE: 16 feet long by 3 feet wide, this recumbent micaceous sandstone slab bisects the axis at 80°, aligning to winter solstice sunrise. Ten feet behind the henge center, it's the only stone of its kind at the site.

BLUESTONES: The method of transport for these nearly ninety, two to four-ton pillars is hotly debated, but whether moved by glacier, human agency, or a little of both, all agree that it was early; some say from the beginning. Used in various configurations throughout the active life of Stonehenge, they came from the rugged Preselli hills in West Wales, 150 miles away. Within the outcrop at Craig Rhosyfellin analysis has determined from where at least one of the bluestones originated, perhaps used in an interim monument before coming to Stonehenge. At present the wider vicinity is being combed for that location, so watch this space!

SOUTH BARROW: Probably built in a later stage of the pre-stone configuration, this feature obscures the remains of a wooden-posted D-shaped structure in addition to three Aubrey Holes. Smaller than the North Barrow, this single-ditched mound was most likely sized to prevent impinging into the Southern Causeway. As will be shown, both represent the moon in its long cycles of 9.3- and 18.6-year major & minor standstills.

STATION STONES: Four sarsen boulders form a rectangle that's perpendicular to the axis. Positioned against the bank, one sat off-center on the North Barrow, another in the middle of the South Barrow. Both barrow stones are now missing while the two others remain in place. These unremarkable rocks are frequently over-looked in the scheme of things, but are now known to play a key role in the stone phase of Stonehenge.

TRILITHONS: *[Greek: Tri + Lithos, or 3-stones.]* Sarsen is among the densest rocks on earth — several times harder than granite — and can still be collected from the Fyfield and Marlborough Downs, 20 miles to the north. Five enormous arches are composed of it, consisting of two standers and a lintel. Formed as a horseshoe, opposing pairs are graduated at 19 and 21 feet, with the Great Trilithon at 26 feet. Each of the four paired sets is dressed so the left side is polished on the inside while the other, though tooled, is rough. This arrangement is open to the summer solstice sunrise, while spacing between the uprights of the Great Trilithon allowed a clear sightline to winter solstice sunset, thought to have held more significance than the June counterpart.

THE SARSEN CIRCLE: Thirty sarsen uprights were mated to thirty joined and seated lintels to create a level, continuous ring. Like the Trilithons, each stone is shaped and worked. More finely crafted on the inside, the circle is designed to allow unobstructed passage of the sun at both solstices. Meticulous laser scans conducted in 2012 indicate that, with the exception of Stone-16 and presumably -15, the two which straddled the winter axis, the quality of the stones decline as they proceed around to the southwest, strongly suggesting that the structure was only intended to be seen publicly from near, or within, the narrow confines of the Avenue.

THE AVENUE: This processional departs the henge and runs straight for about 600 yards, centered on the solstice axis. It then takes an abrupt right at what's known as the *Elbow,* and in a broad southeast curve travels overland to the banks of the River Avon, two miles distant. Unpaved and 90 feet wide, its own ditch and bank mimic the exterior/interior feature of the main structure. Narrowing on its approach to the river, it terminates at the modest West Amesbury Henge, where cremations were conducted for interment in the Aubrey Holes.

Throughout the era of Stonehenge there was no knowledge or wide use of writing, metal or wheels.

An oblique overhead of the Stonehenge complex from the west. The tourist walkway slashes into the henge, obliterating the North Barrow. Faint traces of the Avenue ditches can be seen entering from the upper left, passing under the moveable land bridge. The Heelstone sits between them.

A close crop of the Sarsen Circle from the south. Clearly seen is the horseshoe-shaped Trilithon set, open to the summer solstice sunrise. Of these 5 enormous arches, 3 remain intact, while the Sarsen Circle sits in partial disarray, with only 17 of its 30 stones still standing.

ABOVE: To the left-center of this west side view is the West Trilithon, which collapsed in January 1797, but carefully re-erected in September 1958. In laying on the ground for 161 years, Lintel-158 — among many others — suffered a thrashing from stone-chipping souvenir hunters.

BELOW: Seen from the south, the battered embankment barely rises above the surrounding turf. It was originally 8-feet high. The ditch, first scoured down to 6-feet, is now heavily silted, in places nearly full.

The two entrance stones loom up before us. They are spaced more widely apart for the solstices.

The entrance stones seen from the interior, looking out toward the Heelstone.

Richard Atkinson's excavation of the upper Avenue in the 1950s, looking east. Showcased are the gullies, most likely created by permafrost meltwater, which may have provided powerful motivation for siting Stonehenge at this otherwise unremarkable location.

These red deer antlers were recovered from a ditch section of the henge. Used as picks for prying chalk loose, many were placed in the bottom of the trenches for reasons unknown.

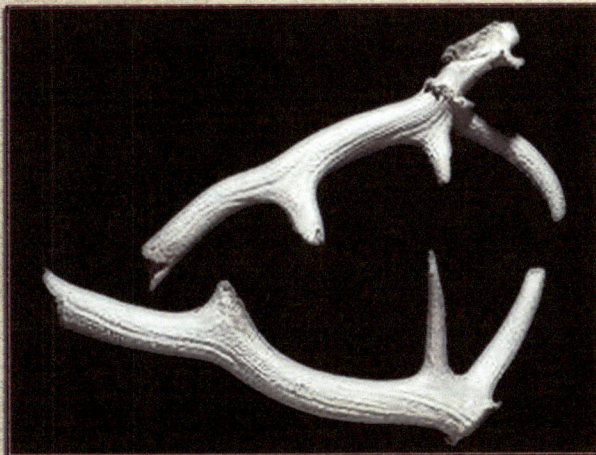

Aubrey Hole-7, re-opened in 2008 to recover the jumble of cremated remains which were dumped there in 1935. Originally excavated from other holes, at least 28 men, women and children have been identified so far.

William Hawley's excavation of the outer area in 1924, showing features around the Heelstone. The socket for Stone-B is seen in the center of the stripe, in addition to some of the grooves. In the distance is the Amesbury-11 Bell Barrow, while the Stonehenge ticket office peeks out from behind the Heelstone. The spiffy, chauffeured automobile no doubt carried well-heeled daytrippers to the site, as the advent of motor vehicles and paved roads made travel easy and inexpensive in the 1920s.

Visitor numbers skyrocketed to 5,000 per year! (Today it's double that on any sunny weekend.)

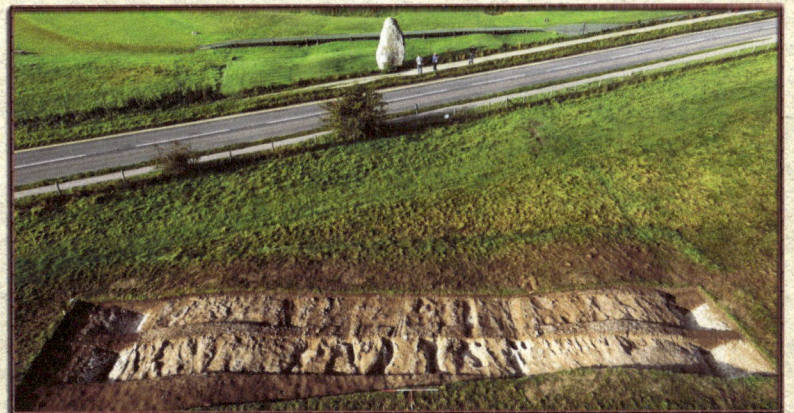

The Avenue striations in 2007. The Heelstone is at top.

Mike Pitts' 1979 discovery of the hole for Stone-97, just a few yards north of the Heelstone. The news was met with excitement by researchers convinced it was the Heelstone's twin. Thirty-nine years later I contend there was only ever one stone and this hole is where it stood before being moved a few centuries later.

Over the years there's been a lot of speculation about how the henge was actually built. Because Stonehenge is among the last Neolithic enclosures, the builders employed techniques similar to those used for a thousand years. Here, the idea displays forethought, has a good engineering principle, and shows how an experienced workforce would articulate the paradigm of a belief system — while being supported by all available evidence.

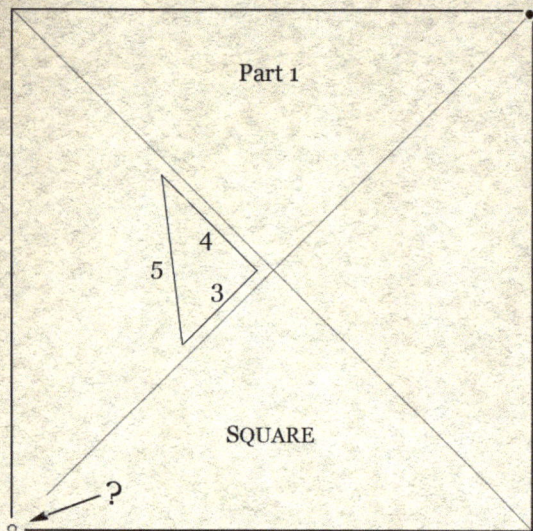

Part 1

4
5
3

SQUARE

?

During the Mesolithic era, the period just prior to the time of our story, the regional landscape was dotted with light forest. As people began to settle in and agriculture was introduced, the woodlands were cleared for farms and homes. The new grassland exposed long gullies in the chalk underbed which coincidently run parallel to the sunline at summer solstice dawn. Being long aware of the sun's significance and its spiraled movement along the horizon over the year, the people undoubtedly deemed this district special — now reinforced by those striations. Over time, several types of structures were built to emphasize these attributes, supported by the reflected, amplified meaning found in every nook and cranny of daily life.

There must have been a couple of big rocks lying near the termination of those peculiar stripes, perhaps having been formed on the spot millions of years before. Workers lifted the biggest of these so the solstice sun would rise directly behind it as seen from the proposed center of the henge. This created the corner of a giant square. A straight run was then made 550 feet along the solstice sunline, and here could have been placed another stone, though it's not known for sure as that area has never been investigated. A center for the entire thing was then paced out, and the right-angle corners of the square could be made using a carpenter's simple 3/4/5 method.

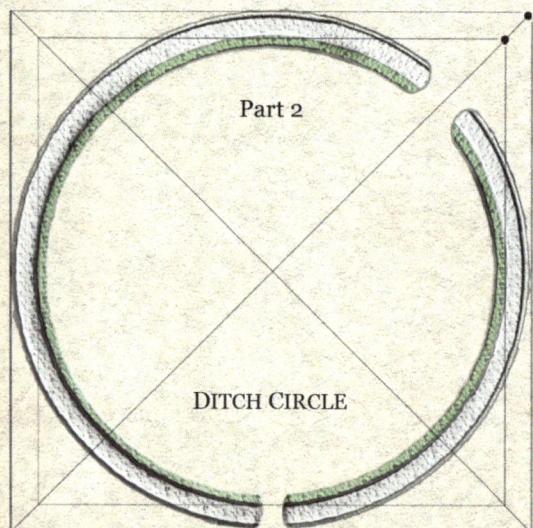

Part 2

DITCH CIRCLE

A second stone was then positioned on the diagonal a short distance from the first, creating boundaries for the henge ditch. 365 feet wide, it was scoured out in segments over years by seasonal gangs, with the spoil cast willy-nilly inside for the bank. Fat, skinny, deep, shallow, there's even a short straight run in the southwest — which incidently infers more than just one gang-boss. There's no denying it's a sloppy job — but it *never* exceeds the square. The oft-proposed stick-and-rope method cannot have been applied here, made painfully obvious by the arbitrary imperfections. But even a quick glance shows they were almost certainly *aiming* for those outer marks.

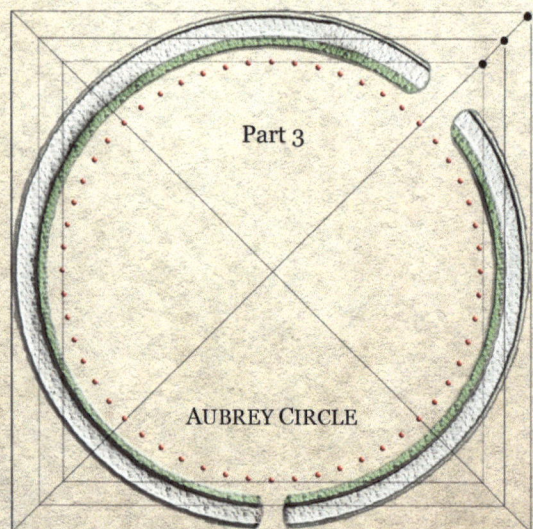

Part 3

AUBREY CIRCLE

A third stone was set an equal distance from the second along the diagonal, creating a corner for the inner square. *This is where the stick-and-rope was used, for the circle it describes is as perfect as could be done using technology available in the late Stone Age.*

It defined where the Aubrey Hole perimeter was to be sited, while such precise effort underscores the importance of those fifty-six mysterious pits.

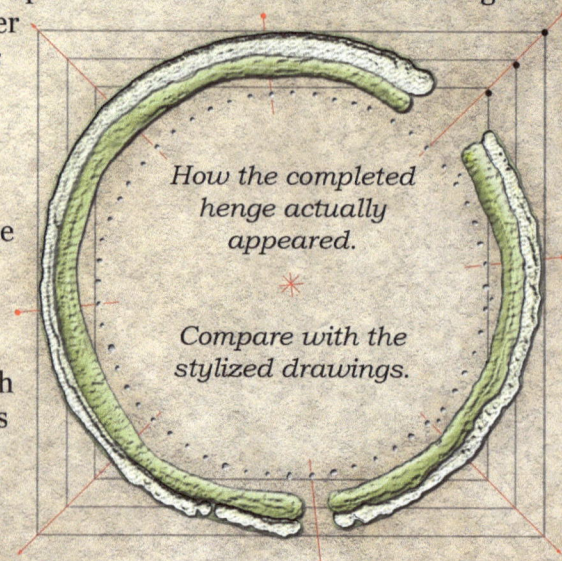

How the completed henge actually appeared.

Compare with the stylized drawings.

Satisfied with the method by which the henge was built, I moved to sequence other elements at the complex. Soon it became obvious that several components appear to be incorrect. Though the axis as plotted aligns with the summer solstice rising at that time, the Aubrey's seem random, meaning they're situated against a background where none of the axes hit. The spacing between holes is sloppy, while the Southern Gap is way out of wack with the natural cardinal. What was going on in there—and why?

I realize that of the many enclosures, long barrows, or henges built around that time, few are aligned to anything, so why should Stonehenge be different? In truth it's an odd-ball structure — not really a henge at all as the bank is *inside* the ditch. I fussed with the cardinals awhile before arriving at the frustrated conclusion that the ignorant barbarians of fifty-one centuries ago were simply careless with the layout.

Labels on diagram: Stone-97, Stone-B, Stone-C, Solar Axis of 5,100 YBP, AH-48, AH-42, false NORTH, AH-56, AH-34, false WEST, false EAST, AH-6, AH-28, false SOUTH, AH-20, AH-14

Scale: 0 10 25 50 75 100 — Scale in Feet

But were they? Let's take a look at some of these nagging curiosities.

The Earth revolves like a spinning top and its tilted axis rolls around the center, taking 26,000 years to describe a cone. This is called Precession of the Equinox. One aspect of the process is that the poles flutter like a ribbon along the cone's outer circumference and this oscillation causes subtle alterations in the pitch of the axis. Though taking centuries to observe on the ground, this shift presents itself as the sun's rise-point sliding east or west over time. So 5,100 years ago the summer solstice occurred about 1.5° further west than it does today.

The rising sun is easy to spot and by using it three people can make a straight line. One with a tall stick stands a hundred yards in the sun's direction, while one with another stick stands between him and the third. As the sun pokes up over the horizon the third person aligns the sticks by directing the second right or left. A mark is kicked in the turf when it's correct. If this is done at solstice you'll have the perfect axis for your layout square.

The builders knew that north was always the same distance above the horizon, and at that time the star Thuban marked this spot rather than Polaris. Like the solar axis, they sighted the line *across* the henge. But Thuban orbited the pole further away from true north than does the present star, so it was west of the actual cardinal.

Then, unlike the primary cardinal and solar alignment, east and west were sighted from the *center* and deter-mined by the sun's rise at vernal equinox or set at autumnal equinox. But the horizons of both have hills in the distance, making those sightlines inaccurate, so the cross cardinals have a dog-leg from one side to the other.

Regardless of this incorrect process, *they* thought it was pretty good, so went out and positioned the Aubreys along those radiants. The errors were compounded by these now-immutable benchmarks, while several other design elements are based on those nodes. Later when they were fixed, the cardinals drifted away from our Aubreys and the sun had slipped a little east — which now leaves us scratching our heads because nothing aligns anymore. I don't believe these flaws in the execution have been previously noticed, demonstrated by the ongoing debate on what these pits were for. Say what you will about the purpose, but this is how they did it.

So then, in this anomalous layout the solar axis begins at S-97, skims offset Stones -B and -C, travels directly over AH-56, through the henge center-point and out over AH-28. The equatorial line hits AH-42 and -14. While north is kissing the barrow, it occults AH-48, passes through the middle, then out over AH-20 to bisect the Southern Gap. East and west do this with -6 and -34. The two sets intersect as they cross the center. So according to the more precise standards of a couple of centuries later, we now see no clear pattern of holes and radiants — all because it's layered over that sloppy original footprint. Innacurate: Yes. Careless: By no means.

Whatever they were up to, the geometry was becoming rather complicated for such oafish brutes!

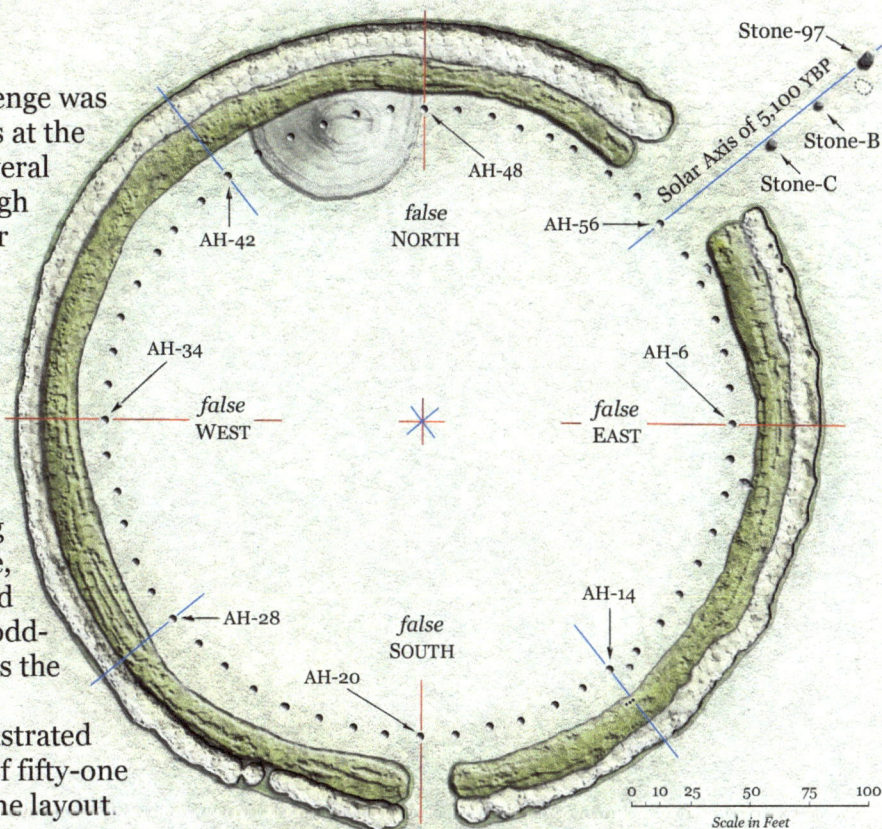

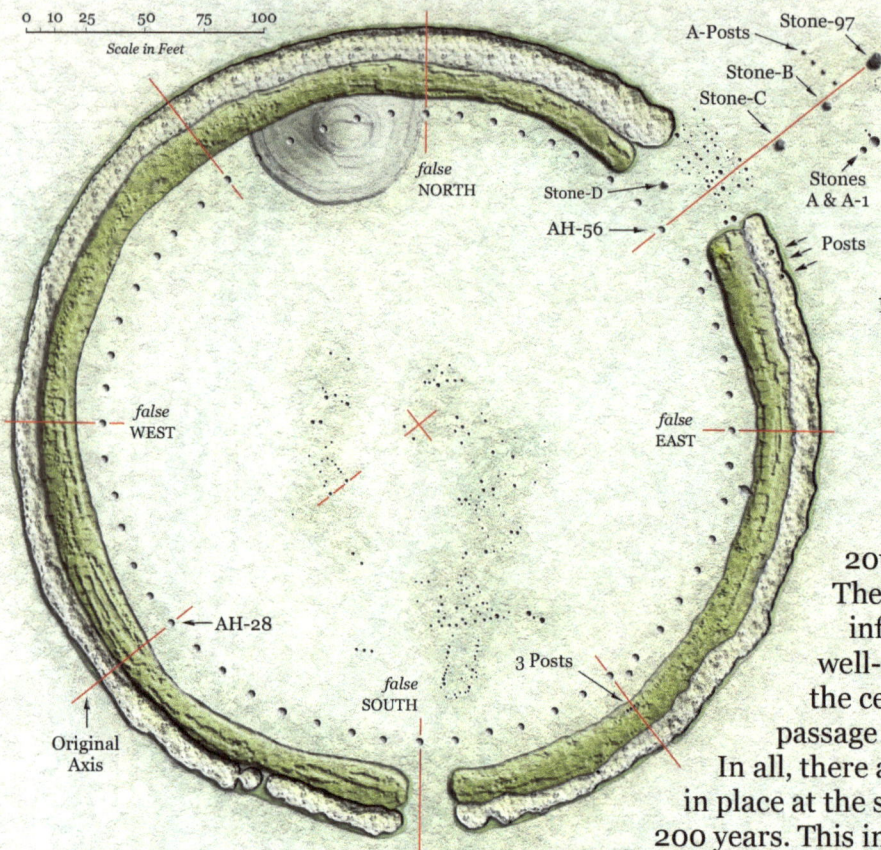

Scale in Feet

0 10 25 50 75 100

A-Posts Stone-97

Stone-B
Stone-C

false NORTH   Stone-D

Stones A & A-1

AH-56

Posts

false WEST

false EAST

AH-28

3 Posts

false SOUTH

Original Axis

Dating the components at Stonehenge is a problem, so a degree of latitude must be given when we make our assumptions. Conversely, whether we know a precise date or not, an understanding of the end purpose will usually give us the sequence from one feature to another. On page 16 we saw the 3 stones in line with the entrance were in place from the start, though others depicted here may not have been. Those play key roles in what we'll see on page 19.

We see several sets of varying-sized post-holes in the interior, discovered during the 20th century. There are also three stoneholes. These posts represent structures whose shapes infer certain functions. For example, there's a well-defined rectangle whose long axis points to the center, and notice the prominent outline of a passage leading directly to the Southern Causeway. In all, there are five or six sets and it's felt that few were in place at the same time, but variously erected over about 200 years. This indicates a honing of the old belief-system.

Notice that there is a dearth of postholes in the northwest. That's because that area has never been investigated, while ground penetrating radar has proved inconclusive. Therefore, whichever theory we select, it's important to bear in mind that we're looking at an incomplete picture of what lies under about half the interior surface.

The Aubrey Holes, called: *X-Holes* when discovered in the 1920s, were also plugged with timber posts, which created a perimeter just inside the bank. Later, though still within this time-frame, these posts were replaced with bluestone pillars whose origin is the Preselli hills in West Wales. The stones must have been imbued with great significance to justify this 150-mile journey. (On-going arguments rage over the method of transport.)

The area out beyond the entrance has been extensively excavated and is well-documented. Firstly, we have the four so-called A-Posts to the west of Stone-97. Three of these are similar in size, while the inner one is smaller and offset, likely due to different times of installation. Planted in a straight line, they roughly align to the henge's equator, though the smaller one doesn't hit the axis. The larger of them may align to gullied striations out on the future Avenue, but I believe they're all very old and were gone by the time the others were emplaced. There may be some connection with, or replacement by, the A-Stones on the opposite side of the axis.

Next up, we see that crazy thicket of posts within the entrance, and a huge volume of work has been done in an attempt to explain what these were. Gerald Hawkins thought they were part of his elaborate eclipse predictor. Mike Pitts suggests they had something to do with a mortuary arrangement. Both Julian Richards and Richard Atkinson thought they were a kind of screening turnstile into the main area. Several others also have good, evidence-based ideas with certain elements in common. But whichever theory we endorse, the facts are that we see six rows of transverse holes along nine longitudinal sets. All appear to have been installed at the same time. A few of these sets seem to be arranged in corridors, but where the old axis passes through, the blank is quite a bit wider than the others, while being flanked by two equidistant posts as it enters. None of the passage sets are parallel, and none are connected in any way to movements of the sun. So where does all this leave us?

Let's return to what has quickly become quite a puzzling annoyance — those pesky Aubrey Holes.

The builders spent lots of effort to ensure that this circle of pits was accurate. Why? No doubt one reason is the layers of cremated human remains placed in or clustered near at least several. Taking what's been excavated and cautiously extrapolating, there may well be upwards of 300 people interred around the site's perimeter.

So it seems the original Stonehenge was, in part, a kind of regional cemetery.
But no cemetery in known history has ever been ruled by the sun.

THE LUNAR STANDSTILLS
How the Moon interacts with features at Stonehenge

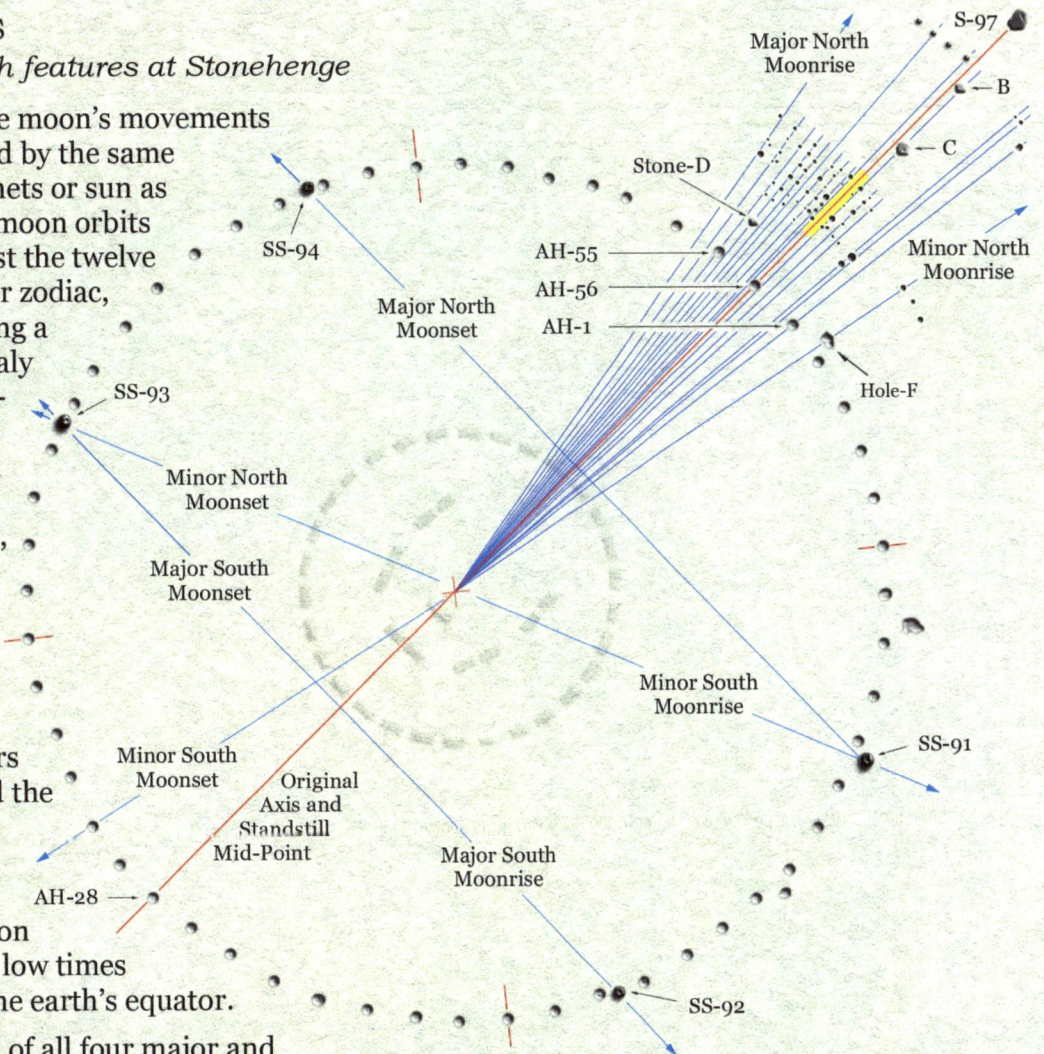

This illustration shows that the moon's movements across the sky are not governed by the same rules as those of the stars, planets or sun as seen from Earth. Because the moon orbits at a more acute 5° angle against the twelve constellations of the ecliptic, or zodiac, it gives the impression of having a wobble in its orbit. This anomaly causes it to rise or set at different points along the horizon during the year, often within a single monthly cycle. This complex motion is predictable, but out of sync with the more stately movements of the sun.

Due to this wobble, the moon has a long-term cycle which takes it farther north or south than at other times. This occurs alternately every 9.3 years and the process is known as the Major or Minor Lunar Standstill. At high times the moon will rise and set on a point of the horizon that the sun never reaches. At low times it does this below and above the earth's equator.

Shown here is the progression of all four major and minor lunar standstills that can be seen from the center of the monument or a Station Stone. Suffice it to say that there's other contrived elements within the build which also appear to be oriented with certain aspects of the lunar metonic cycle. The solstice sunline naturally occurs at the mid-point between major and minor northern moonrise, but to the people then it must have seemed pre-ordained.

A trend at the entrance shows unobstructed sightlines emerging from the center, along what appear to be 'Light Corridors', over and through which the moon could be observed at different stages of the north standstill rising. Realistically, these sightlines — and therefore the mysterious posts themselves — can have no other meaning. While lunar incidences at Stonehenge have been previously noted by Newall, Burl, Hawkins, Dunn and others, the entrance posthole association has not been widely published.

What becomes obvious is, with the eventual introduction of the Trilithons and Stone Circle, all central lunar sightlines were interrupted four or five hundred years later when solar influence took precedence. People today frequently can't, literally, see past the stones, and this may be why the lunar relationships are seldom noticed.

The people who built Stonehenge clearly knew all about these short- mid- and long-term cycles, so they were liberally embedded into the complex. On observing the orbital peculiarities and monthly phasing — then throw in the occasional solar or lunar eclipse — it's easy to see how those folks would have held the moon in esteem.

But what kind of esteem?

Sun is strong and brilliant. His actions are constant and dependable. Though his lessons can be harsh, he is always open-handed and fair. His beautiful, bountiful Earth wife and all their children are amply provided for. Sun also has a sister, the dark Princess Moon. Forever in his shadow, she has no life-giving credentials. Tricky and petulant, she is jealous of her brother's radiance and spiteful of his wife's beauty. Ruling from the night, she secretly governs all females in the world, directing their monthly cycles of renewal. Only the dead are entrusted to her care and she performs this odious task by ushering them into the darkness. Ever capricious, she must remain under constant surveillance — which is first among the things this place was intended to do.

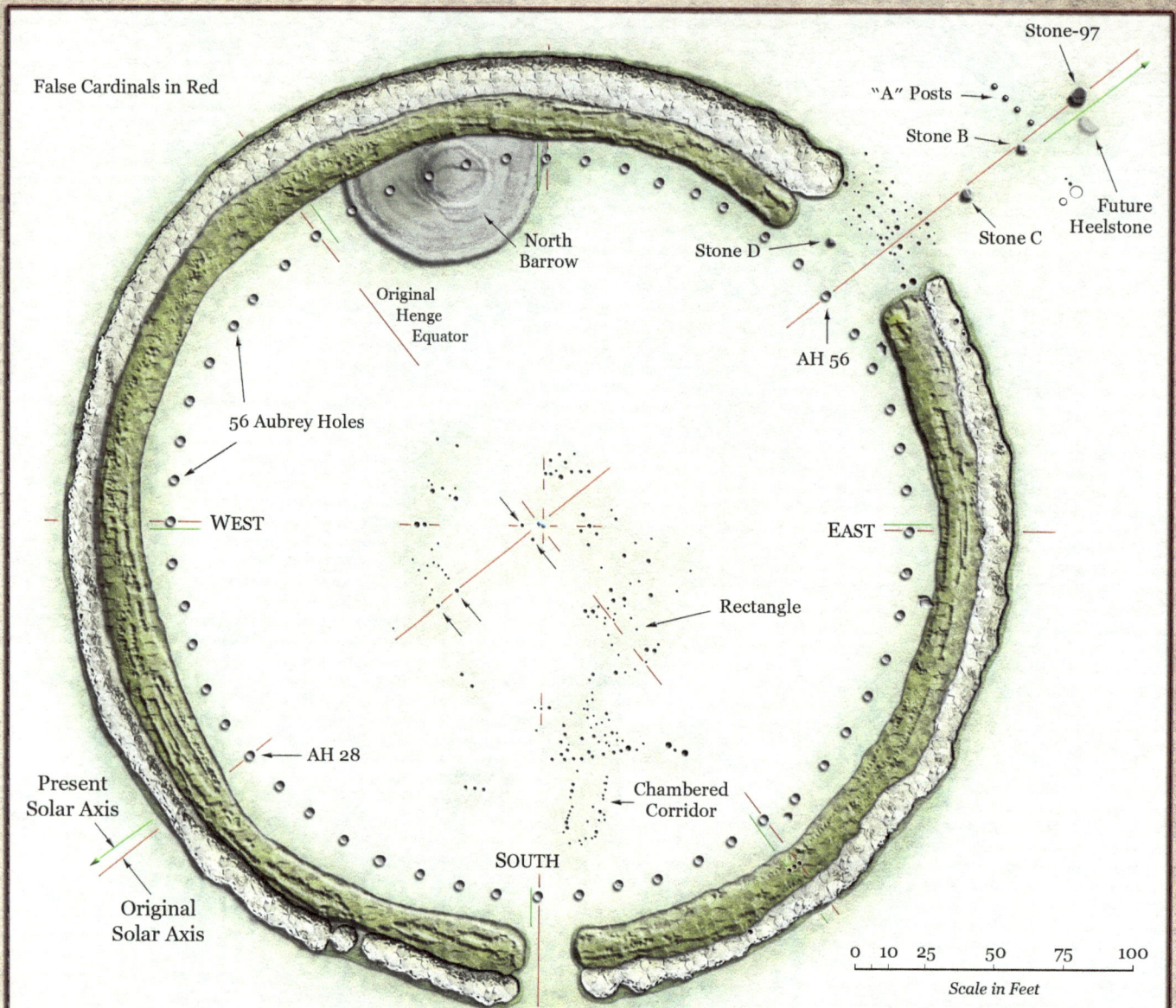

STONEHENGE c.5,000 — 4,800 BP.
Showing Stones and Postholes which existed during this period.

False Cardinals in Red

Stone-97

"A" Posts

Stone B

Future Heelstone

North Barrow

Stone D

Stone C

Original Henge Equator

AH 56

56 Aubrey Holes

WEST

EAST

Rectangle

AH 28

Present Solar Axis

Chambered Corridor

SOUTH

Original Solar Axis

0 10 25   50   75   100
Scale in Feet

Postholes at the Entrance correspond with the moon. The interior holes are a series of five or six structures which didn't all exist at the same time, but were added to or subtracted from over a period of about 200 years. Notice that at least four of the holes have unequivocal associations with the original axis and equator before slipping off-kilter when the corrected emphasis went from lunar to solar. It also suggests there was more than one cultural influence between this and the stone phase.

The 'A' Posts out by S-97 were no doubt gone by the time the entrance holes were made, while the four stones shown remained in place, as the three outside are components of the original layout square. Then stones -B, -C and -D, clearly associated with the moon, were eventually removed and used else-where. Stone-E and the Slaughter Stone are candidates. S-97, shifted to the Heelstone spot, was offset to the new axis and socketed at a different depth so the top would eclipse the arcing sunrise in June.

Unknown are any post- or stone holes which may have occurred in the north and northwest, as this area of the henge field has never been fully investigated. By the same token, other than in the previous discussions of rise- and set points, neither moon nor sun interact with these directions in any way.

The North Barrow is shown as it is a pre-existing structure, the purpose of which is unknown. True Cardinals are shown in green, but it's questionable if the builders ever determined them correctly, as there's a nagging sense of 'Close Enough is Good Enough' attached to some of the early calculations.

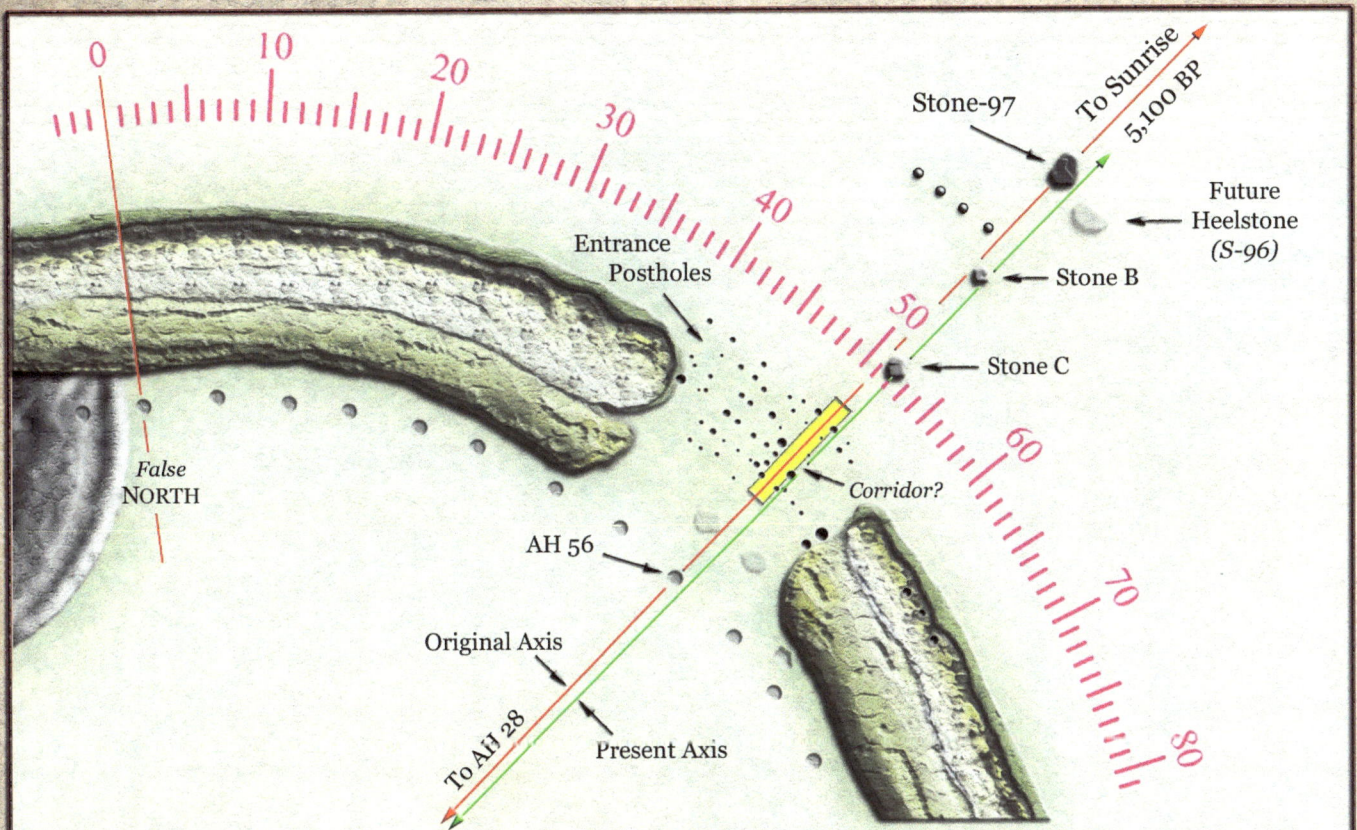

The original axis at Stonehenge centered on Stone-97 and passed uninterrupted through the northeast causeway. Notice how it whisks by Stones -B & -C, crosses directly over Aubrey 56, travels through the center of the monument and then out over Aubrey 28. The entrance postholes seem to accommodate a corridor for this line, which is ushered by two large, equidistant uprights.

The sunline occurs at 51° from north; one hint among several that the builders had figured out the Earth is a sphere. By using simple ground observations they could have plotted the cardinals — no stars or magnets required. This tells us they were aware of Stonehenge's latitude on the globe regardless of the slightly incorrect compass orientation. But because these things were so poorly determined at the beginning, they became a nuisance when it came time to rehabilitate the site.

Later, the sun's rise-point invariably slipped 1° east, so a green arrow shows the new sightline at 52°. At midpoint on the future Avenue, it now bumps into several obstacles while missing the two key Aubrey Holes altogether. The fresh sunline, true cardinals, along with the henge's corrected equator, created a different center for the monument, and this tells us it cannot be original.

During the stone remodel a few hundred years on, they not only addressed the old mistakes, but honed the sophisticated motive they were attempting to convey. It was no longer a fear of the sun's disappearance, but security in its permanence. As its original placement blocked the sunrise, the builders rotated Stone-97 into the Heelstone position. In several instances, it was the sightline that became important, so we see a number of offset stones at the complex. That said, in the Heelstone's case it didn't matter where the sun rose as long as it peened off the crown to cast a long, pointed shadow through the Circle, deep into the Trilithon receptacle and onto the Altar Stone.

A two-dimensional map gives a picture. The three-dimensional landscape lends texture. But time's fourth dimension factors sequence and only here can we resolve intent. The chalk reveals the beginning, middle and end of a progression, showing that Stonehenge wasn't constructed as a finished monument in stasis, but crafted over time by a culturally morphing people whose early mistakes were corrected by deeper understanding and a more experienced world view. Within this new interpretation is the unending cycle of life, not death, with an equal role for male and female.

We interrupt the silky flow of this riveting narrative to bring you important information concerning potential inaccuracies in measurements at Stonehenge.

The photo below is a postcard from 1961 and shows the condition of Stonehenge following the extensive restoration and excavations in the late 1950s. Clearly seen are the marks where the beds of herringbone railroad ties served to protect the surface from heavy equipment, even though we still see tire tracks from the various necessary truck traffic. A service building and a few errant piles of chalk remain at the upper left.

A footnote curiosity is that even after the extensive reconstruction work we can still detect the nearly full contour of the North Barrow, seen at about the 2 o'clock position on the henge circumference. Ironically, it was almost completely obliterated a few years later with the introduction of the tourist walkway.

Notice the partial ring of variously sized white dots swinging around from west to northeast in a partial circle. These are concrete caps set by workmen after Hawley's excavations in the 1920s, marking the position of the 32 Aubrey Holes he'd investigated. The caps are still there, though now mostly unseen below new turf.

Fast-forward to the present.
Because different map makers have been slightly inconsistent over the course of the last few years, there has been a muted call to inspect those caps and verify the precise location of the 56 Aubrey Holes once and for all.

In 1950 Richard Atkinson went around the west & northwest perimeter of the bank, stuck a half-inch thick steel re-bar into the ground, said: "Here's one!" and marked the position on the 1919 Hawley-amended survey map. Dr Rosamund Cleal took that information, codified it in 1994, and we're using it now.

Is this information accurate to the micro arc-second? I'm confident it's not.
Is it good enough to illustrate what the builders' intention for the holes were? With little question.
If the hole locations are off by ten feet we have a problem, yes.
If they're out by two, or maybe even three feet? Not so much — and it's unlikely they're out that badly.

When the apex of our crafting ability is a fluted ceramic pot or chipped flint arrowhead, observations translated into complex metaphor must be physically realized with a certain degree of forgiveness for potentially wide plus/minus variables. When the priest or whomever said: "Thou shalt dig 56 holes!" I have a hunch that the guys chopping and shoveling with antler picks and shoulder blades were just trying to get the job done.

In attempts to understand the multi-layered physical and symbolic intention of the Aubrey Holes, what's shown on various maps is enough for us to make plenty of good deductions based on reasonable accuracy.

We now return to the regularly scheduled timeline of our Stonehenge tale …

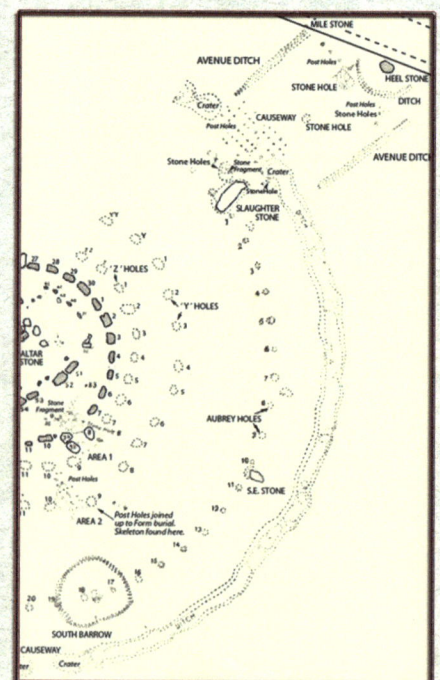

AUBREY HOLES DIVIDE THE SEASONS

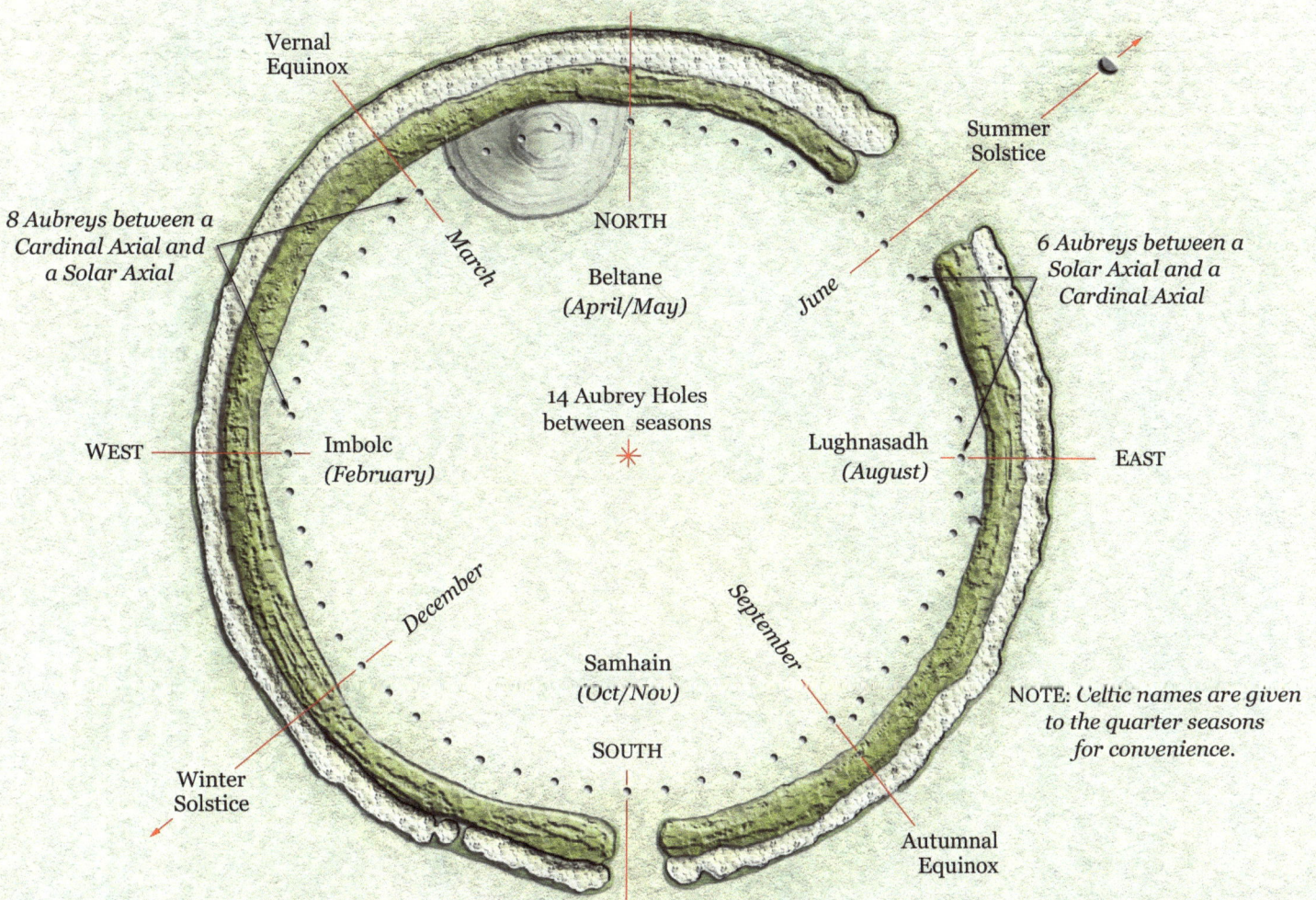

Vernal Equinox

8 Aubreys between a Cardinal Axial and a Solar Axial

Summer Solstice

6 Aubreys between a Solar Axial and a Cardinal Axial

March

June

NORTH

Beltane
(April/May)

14 Aubrey Holes
between seasons

WEST

Imbolc
(February)

Lughnasadh
(August)

EAST

December

September

Samhain
(Oct/Nov)

NOTE: *Celtic names are given to the quarter seasons for convenience.*

SOUTH

Winter Solstice

Autumnal Equinox

One metonic cycle of the moon = 18.6 years, starting at high standstill, through low standstill, then back again. Only at the completion of this cycle will the moon ever rise in the same location, position, and phase. 18.6 x 3 = 55.8, or pretty close to 56. Twenty-eight days a month in a 13-month year, gives us 56 weeks; leaving one leftover day at the end. This creates a 6.5-day week and may be why, as time-keepers, the Aubrey's are roughly 6.5-degrees apart. *(This leap day might have been more party time at winter solstice?)*

Rounding down, one lunar week = one Aubrey Hole. A mirror to the sky's orbit, the system rotated clockwise, beginning with June as marked by Aubrey-56, and December by Aubrey-28. Traveling from the solstice sunrise, the number of Aubrey's to cardinal east is six 'weeks', or the quarter-season Lughnasadh in August. From the autumnal equinox, count six more holes and wind up at south in Samhain, or October. Winter solstice plus six = Imbolc, or February in west, and from vernal equinox to Beltane in the north, or April/May.

The time between the 4 solar axes is 14 Aubreys, or the weeks between full seasons. In this configuration, the sun becomes the placeholder for summer, autumn, winter, spring, while the cardinals note the intervals between. Both sets are stamped into the system and the trend appears to have emerged from the initial layout.

Counting days with the Aubrey's against observations of stellar positions would give them a particular seasonal change virtually to the hour — such as we do. *(Gerald Hawkins was on the right track.)* This is why all those stones and posts at, and beyond the entrance were so vital. It was how the builders were able to precisely record the lunar standstills, which was the basis for their entire calendar for almost nineteen years at a stretch. So we have bluestone pillars in the Aubreys for the stars, with the posthole and stone arrangements at the entrance for the moon. *(The interior of the henge would be Earth, a concept later adapted into the Sarsen Circle.)*

FOOTNOTE: In the beginning, the sun set in Gemini at winter solstice. Due to precession of the equinox, it now sets in Pisces. *(A hundred and twenty-odd years from now it will be Aquarius.)* This inexorable shifting of the constellations would have been noticeable over 500 years, so any subsequent recalibration of the system could be precisely maintained by observations across an elevated circular structure, such as level stone lintels.

*Illustrator Peter Dunn brings dusty, dry facts and figures to life
with fleshed, interpretive reconstructions of many Neolithic sites.*

This depiction of Stonehenge integrates what's in the evidence with how it most likely looked during an early time frame. Though the North Barrow is omitted, we see other elements we've discussed to this point. Viewed from the south, this is c.4,900 years ago and exposed chalk from the recently completed ditch and bank still gleams white in the sun. We can see the various segment-scours in the ditch, caused by separate clan or family gangs digging in different areas.

Quality oversight seems not to have been an issue, as there are eight of these segments in the near areas, each dug to diverse widths and depths. Although the northwest circumference has never been excavated, it's thought there might be as many as 22 of these 'Craters', as William Hawley called them. This method of ditch digging was not uncommon and tells us that few were scoured during one episode.

Known to have taken decades to finish, these projects no doubt became robust competitions over time. I like to think there was rivalry between the groups, like popular sports contests today. *"Alright ladies and gents, the two big teams this year are the unbeaten Cursus Chalk Biters against the upstart Avebury Stone Haulers, so you know it's gonna be a tough match. There's the refs handing out picks and shovels — and here we go!"*

At the top right we see Stones -97, -B, and -C, along with the A-Posts strung out across the axis. Inward is that seemingly crazy thicket of posts at the entrance. The Aubreys are plugged with bluestone pillars, used as grave markers as well as that clever moon calendar. Brought 150 miles from Wales, they may have come from a previous stone circle there. Now here they sit, stoically casting afternoon shadows. Many people appear clustered along the interior chambered corridor and at various points around the perimeter, though oddly, few are seen within the reaches of the henge itself.

In the center of the henge field are two posts standing alone, straddling the axis. The recumbent Altar Stone, still years in the future, will lay directly behind this position. The two postholes, discovered in 1953, tell us that this location was of key importance. For whatever reason, the Altar Stone made it permanent. Both older posts and newer stone are equally bisected by the original axis, but when the Heelstone was moved to its present position, the slab itself wasn't shifted, so the sightline is now slightly off-center across it. Recently noticed, it's cocked at 80° to the axis, aligning with winter solstice sunrise.

Though elements which existed at Stonehenge are rarely in question, it's the sequence in which they occur that show a transition from impermanent wood to everlasting stone. Though the time between an addition or subtraction of features isn't known with certainty, we can still show a progression of what's sensible. This is the beginning of the stone era, but there's no evidence to indicate exactly how those changes evolved. Cleverly tucked into this drastic visual overhaul we also see a few subtle changes.

Over the course of years the people who dug the ditch and raised the posts went about their lives with moon observances, burying their cremated dead and the other trappings of daily life. During this time, people came and went from near and far, trading goods, exchanging tools, techniques, passing information — generally doing the same things we do today, albeit at a slower pace. Ideas also came and went and we see this in their tools, pottery, and ornamentation. In some cases we even detect a few indirect links on how they interpreted the world's workings.

NORTH

Shifted Stone-97

WEST

EAST

SOUTH

0 10 25   50   75   100

Scale in Feet

Immigrating from the continent, the Beaker Folk take the name from the shape of their distinctive pottery, which resembles — no joke — beakers. They brought new technology, big ideas and fresh blood. Some argue that their introduction was a kind of swift invasion, but I believe the inevitable blending of cultures happened over time and was welcomed. While the Beakers still honored the dead, their focus was more about life. The sun brings life, so with the development of a new cultural foundation we see the shift to a much more pleasant way of looking at things, and this gently closed the door on the long-lived Windmill Hill people.

Unfortunately, in spite of this new chapter, Stonehenge as it stood was only regionally relevant, concerning itself with routine commemorations of death and the moon. So here we have this big old graveyard with lots of things going for it, but which had been laid out so 'badly' that it was going to be difficult to re-fit to a new purpose. The newcomers did what any group would when faced with a daunting task which would bleed resources away from farming, hunting and all the other imperatives.

They abandoned it without a second look back.

We find shrubs and small trees growing in the previously well-tended ditch and on the bank. It's possible that some of the posts were left in place to rot. A hundred years passed before their grandchildren returned, bringing to bear an arsenal of clever ideas and a workforce enabled by settling to allocate time for the repurposing of this hallowed site. First, that big rock out front had to be moved to mark the new emphasis of solstice, while Stones -B and -C were probably moved to straddle the axis at the entrance. This means that though the Aubreys may have remained in use as a traditional calendar, the new layout threw other lunar aspects off kilter. With the makeover from a moon-centered death motif, the sun became the principle time-keeper.

Then those folks went 20 miles north, selected fifteen slabs of sarsen and spent perhaps ten years shaping and polishing the five Trilithons, which were erected in their distinctive horseshoe assembly. The Altar Stone, no doubt placed previously, remained where it was, so it's off-center to the new axis. It lies at 80° to the sunline and aligns with winter solstice sunrise. Bluestones, removed from the Aubreys, were arranged in a crescent around the Trilithons. At least four of these were shaped with tenons with mortised lintels fixed to them, creating a corridor through which summer solstice dawn was ushered. These oddball stones remain on-site.

Due to the unique use of huge shaped stones and a widely recruited workforce, Stonehenge probably entered cultural renown around this time.

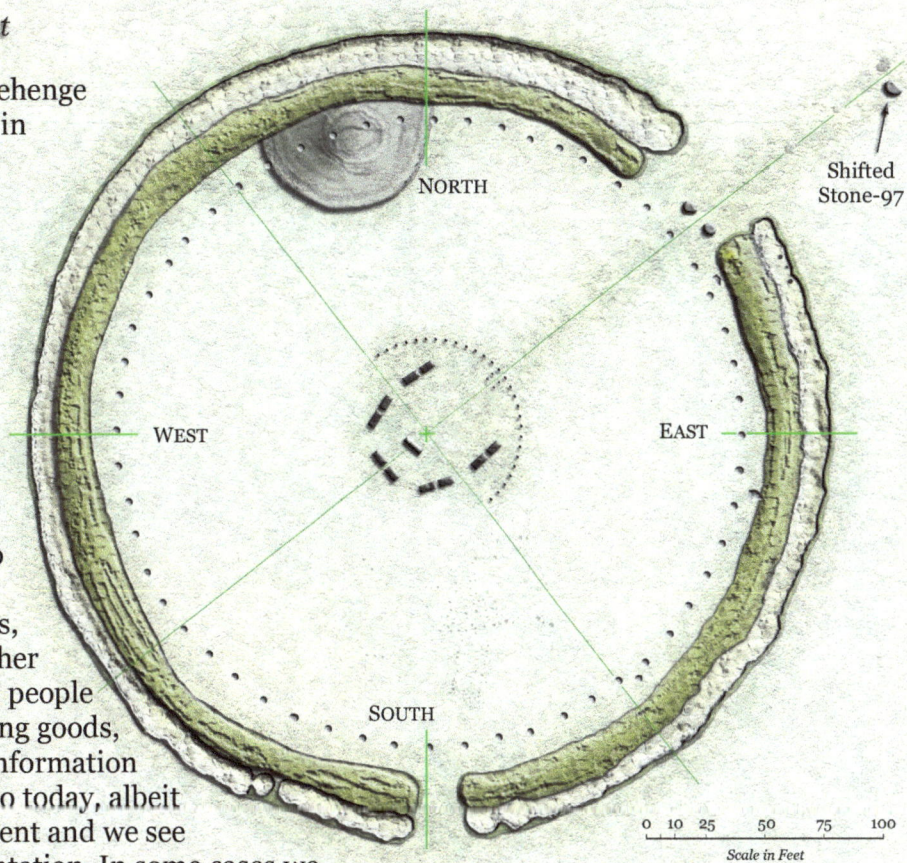

The West Trilithon seen from the outside. It collapsed in 1797 but was re-erected in 1958.

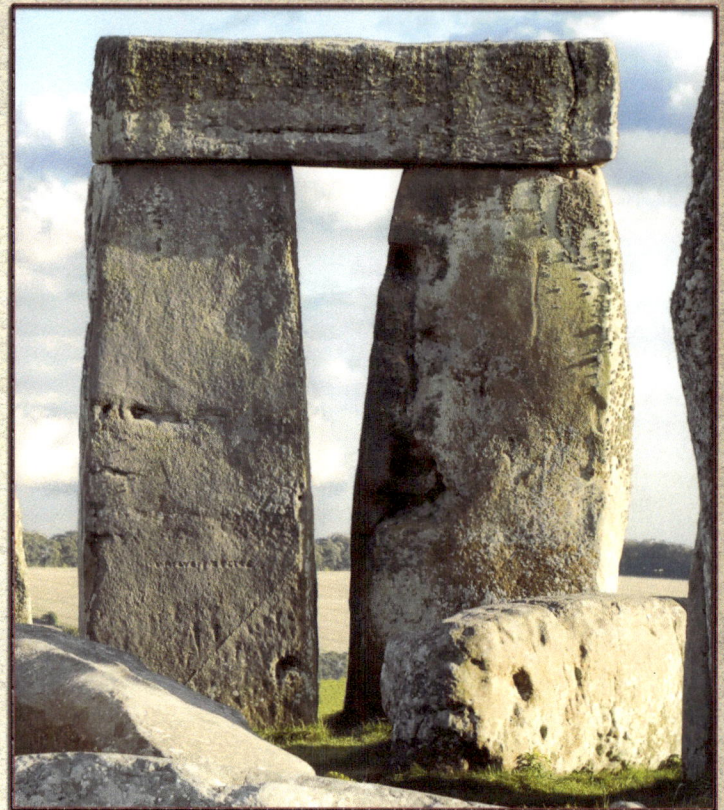

I believe the South Trilithon was the second of the five sets to be raised.

Of the five Trilithons at Stonehenge, three remain intact. Probably raised a hundred years before the Sarsen Circle, each of the huge paired stones is tapered — mere inches apart at the ground, while up to three feet at the lintels. A long-standing curiosity becomes apparent on observing that, seen from the interior, the left stone is more finely crafted than the right. This invites any number of interpretations, but a recent suggestion, in keeping with my own theory, says they most likely represent male and female counterparts of equal status.

The East Trilithon has never been excavated.

As demonstrated to varying degrees, the lintels were originally dressed out with squared corners, plain to see on L-154 of the South Trilithon, and to a lesser extent, -152 of the East Trilithon. Remaining high on their lofty perches, neither were subjected to the ravages of banal, hammer-wielding souvenir hunters over the centuries.

Conversely, the lintel for the West Trilithon, L-158, lay prone across its two fallen standers for 161 years and took an unmitigated thrashing before the entire stack was carefully re-erected by Richard Atkinson's team in 1958. All of its accessible edges are now rounded and irregular. Fortunately, only a few minor incidences of damage have occurred since 1865.

Arguably the premiere Neolithic site in the world, it's no surprise that Stonehenge has been extensively invest-igated for hundreds of years in the past. But not entirely. For all the digging, adjusting and rooting around in various places at the complex, other than by weather, the East Trilithon has remained unscathed — seen now nearly the same as it was when erected 46 centuries ago.

ABOVE: *The bottom half of Stone-55 of the Great Trilithon. Notice the extruded heel on its lower end. Working against a predetermined height and an apparent scarcity of the appropriate length of raw material, the stone was shaped this way as it was much too short. Socketed only four feet down, nearly half its original mass had to be removed to create that feature.*

Sadly, none of this enormous effort worked out well in the end.

Coming in at forty tons apiece, the pair are the tallest of all the sets, but unlike the others, both were carefully polished on all sides. Logic suggests they were the first of the five arches to be erected.

LEFT: *Stone-56 of the Great Trilithon. The tallest single standing stone in the UK, it is 31 feet in total length and 23 feet up from the turf. When sister S-55 came down, the falling lintel, seen in the foreground, yanked -56 by its prominent tenon to begin the slowly increasing lean which made it popular for centuries. The first of 21 stones to be adjusted, it was righted in September 1901 and set into a now-controversial concrete envelope. It will never move again.*

BELOW: *Stones -60 and -59 of the North Trilithon. Notice the concrete infill at -60's base. In fear of its potential collapse on freely*

wandering visitors, the upright was straightened and the fill poured in 1960. We now know that it was raised with this vacancy as it was. (A broom closet?)

The spines on broken Stone-59 show the intense labor by endless scrubbing with heavy sarsen hammerstones. Was it intended to look this way, or were they in a hurry to get the final Trilithon in place?

27

NORTH

WEST

EAST

SOUTH

0 10 25   50   75   100

Scale in Feet

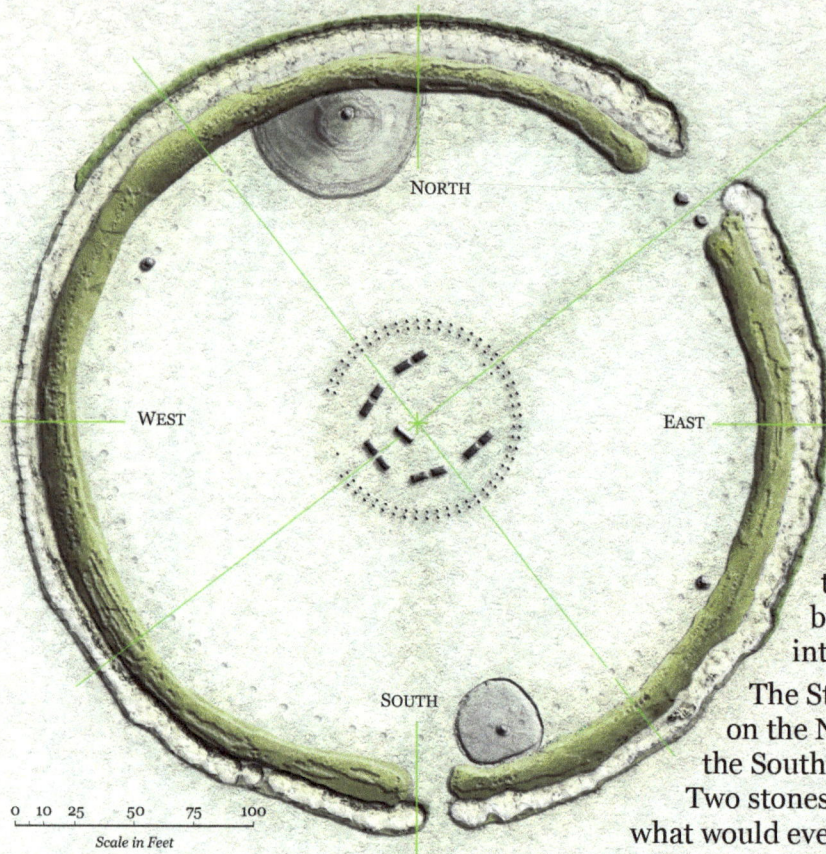

It might be said this period of building is a continuation of the previous, but a quick review shows some subtle differences which indicate a honing of ideas with a view to what was coming in future. The true cardinals are standard now and all is established against the new solstice axis. The crescent of blue-stones has become a double circle, these dumbell-shaped scours now known as the 'Q & R Holes'. There is a new barrow in the south, laid partially over the bank. Only two-thirds the size of its counterpart, the dimension and single-ditched design is some-thing of a mystery. I believe the *location* was theme-critical and the builders were prevented by their belief system from intruding too deeply into the still-relevant Southern Causeway.

The Station Stones probably date to this time, as -94 on the North Barrow is offset, while -92 is centered on the South Barrow, suggesting they were complimentary. Two stones remain at the henge's entrance: Stone-E and what would eventually become known as the Slaughter Stone.

Stone-E, on the west side of the axis, is long gone, but the other remains as a fallen remnant. The depression in which it lies may reflect a failed effort to bury it. Called *slighting*, the practice was usually reserved for objects in the way of roads or buildings — common at Avebury where many stones were buried or reused. Conversely, William Stukeley reports living memory of this stone as upright, so perhaps it fell on its own. Excavated by Cunnington and Colt-Hoare in 1812, as a courtesy to future archaeologists, a fine bottle of port was stashed underneath, recovered by William Hawley in 1920. Sadly, the cork had disintegrated and its contents ruined.

The Aubrey Holes have been out of service as reliquaries for at least a hundred years and are fading into the ground. In my view, their continued use as lunar week-markers is unlikely, as the South Barrow obscures three of them. The ditch was then scoured out and that peculiar east ditch extension was made at this time. It now nearly kisses the axis, but there is no apparent rationale for the procedure. After this, all activity at the henge's bank and ditch ceased and they are never again attended, remaining neglected until the modern age.

Another subtlety in evidence is an odd feature known as the Counterscarp Embankment. Acting as a kind of partial exterior rim, it proceeds less than halfway around the northern and eastern circumference. Until now there seemed to be no logical reason for it to exist. It's presumed that the extra material from the ditch cleaning and extension was used to create it, but these efforts — particularly the overcut — are difficult to explain.

So then, at the place where Sister Moon was once studiously watch-dogged, we now have a balanced triad with Father Sun and Mother Earth. Life is being emphasized, but with cogent recognition of its impermanence. Using shaped stone as a medium to celebrate life was a departure from the traditional, and though Wood/Life, Stone/Death is not an uncommon theme in the Neolithic, here we witness it in a much broader scope — with Moon and Sun performing their elaborate dances around a caring Mother — not discreetly, but together in a complex minuet against the breathtaking backdrop of those massive sarsen skyscrapers.

Overarching concepts had come into play which looked forward to the future, rather than back into the past. While the Trilithons certainly represented the male & female aspects of life, they probably did not specifically represent the ancestors, as is often suggested. This set was a collective manifestation of the verdant, vibrant Earth-Wife resolutely joining with her brilliant Sun-Husband. Meanwhile, their puny, barely consequential human by-products were grudgingly ushered through their brief little lives by Sun's tricky, capricious, and still relentlessly monitored Sister — her mean-spirited pranks acknowledged, but forever kept in close check.

Within this coldly balanced reality, it's the people who became symbolic — not the other way around.

28

It might be the double circle of bluestones remained in place while the sarsen ring was erected. I think their proximity would have interfered with the monumental work and were likely removed for the sake of expediency. Perhaps disassembled in sections, they were then replaced with the famous orthostats. With skill unmatched for 2,000 years, the Circle is nearly perfect and the lintels sit level to the curve of the earth.

There had been debate on whether the ring was ever completed, as there's never been any evidence for Stones -17 or -18 in the southwest segment. During the brutally hot July 2013, sharp-eyed custodians Tim Daw and Simon Banton detected the outline of what are called parchmarks in the turf, right where the two stones should sit. Marks like these are common in chalk downs, formed when rain sinks deep into the original holes, leaving the grass above dry and browned. They frequently occur at many sites during heat waves, including this one, but these two had never been seen before and this threw any number of related theories into question. I duly confess to being a proponent of one such idea.

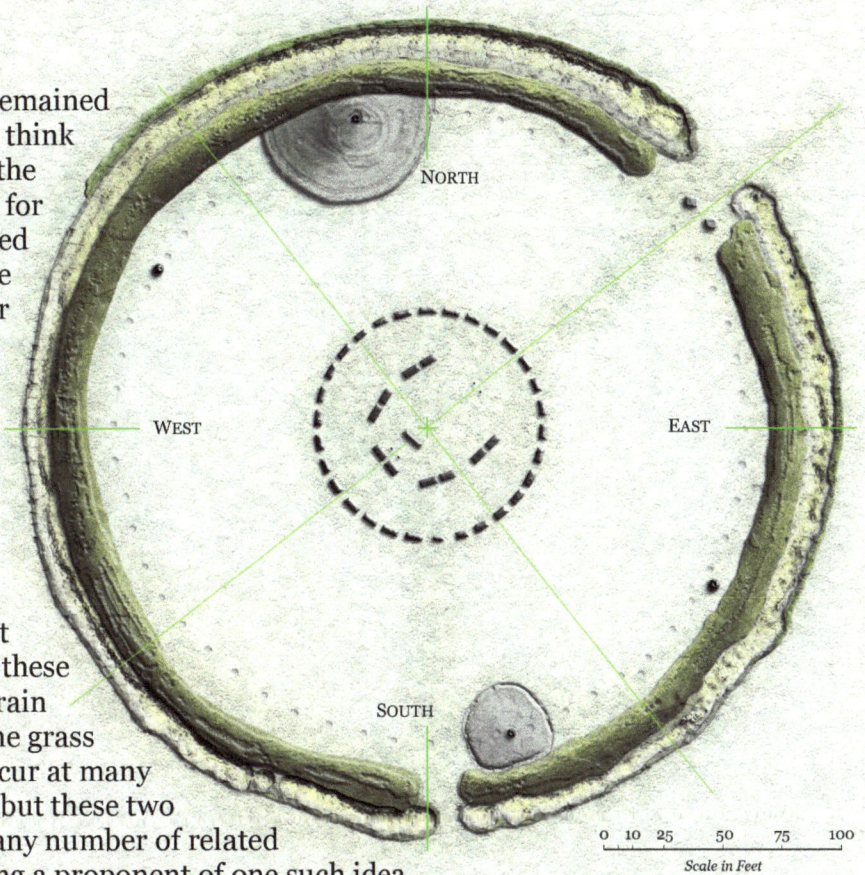

NORTH

WEST

EAST

SOUTH

| 0 | 10 | 25 | 50 | 75 | 100 |

Scale in Feet

At the top of the list among the things that make the Citadel unique is that each of its exterior stones is shaped all around and carefully polished on the inside. While the Trilithons were erected with relative rapidity, it appears that the Circle may have taken up to a hundred years to complete. A few hundred feet to the north is a site where the slabs were delivered and worked, where today, winter ice and ground burrowing creatures frequently bring rock shards to the surface; a testament to the enormous labor of forty-five centuries ago.

Using the raw material at hand lent a certain degree of difficulty, as the lengths of stone vary considerably. Constrained by a predetermined height out of the ground, the sockets were all dug to a different depth. Those at the northeast, or front, are seated quite well, but as we pass to the rear, we find many that are not so carefully planted. This may have been another contributing factor as to why several have collapsed over time.

It has recently been concluded that the Sarsen Circle was most likely intended to be viewed only from the northeast entrance, and perhaps this helps explain some of the less-impressive stones toward the back.

Be that as it may, common to all is that each stone is tapered and all are laid out on-center around the circumference, meaning their position had been established from the middle of the stone rather than the distance between them. This ensured accurate placement along the radius, regardless of any variations in width.

A subtle feature at the complex is found in the topography of the site. Stonehenge doesn't sit on perfectly level ground, but on a very gentle downslope. To accommodate this grade, the stones on the eastern side are socketed higher, ensuring that the lintels remain level, today out only one-half inch over the width of the diameter.

Notice one stone is more slender than all the others. Centered on the old south line, Stone-11 has resisted all efforts to define it. Though S-10 and -12 each have tenons on them, how did a lintel sit on this punky thing?

Each upright has two tenons at either end of their saddle, with the lintel mortises fitted to them — to the point of shaving the underside of some to maintain a level top surface. Each of the sixty butts are clipped at a 6° angle, aimed at the center. Then, alternating tongue-in-groove lock joints were fashioned into the ends to arrest any shifting. Additionally, all were curved inside and out so that when set they would simulate an unbroken ring.

These involved shaping and jointing techniques are common in wood and have been widely used by carpenters from time immemorial. Both difficult and time consuming even for craftsmen today with the use of power tools, at Stonehenge such exacting results were produced with only hand-mauls and crude balls of stone, banging ceaselessly on one of the hardest raw materials in the world. Pretty remarkable if you ask me ...

I think we can agree the Sarsen Circle is the most intriguing feature at Stonehenge, as well as the thing it is most commonly identified with. Though these stones are dwarfed in mass by a hundred other examples, no other Neolithic structure in the world exhibits such careful shaping or precise placement of its orthostats. Seemingly selected for their individual characteristics, each stands unique in the circle, but together unify its entire design. The graded layers of polishing alone sets them apart from efforts elsewhere, while the clever system used to erect them only serves to reinforce our respect for the builders' skill and imagination.

When the apex of engineering technology is a log roller and rope made from the cambium layer of tree bark, our wonder grows exponentially. Years might be spent discussing the *reason* this structure exists, but when tracking concept to result, it has few equals. Additionally, this could not have been achieved by the use of forced labor, as the workmanship is far too good. As in Egypt, there may have been an institutional working class.

One by one the raw materials were delivered by circuitous route — itself a mammoth task — to the work station a short distance north of the site. Ground radar shows fields of chipped sarsen surrounding blank rectangular shapes, indicating where the stones lay while being worked. Sarsen mauls and hammerstones were used to both rough-out then smooth any flaws, banging and scraping, perhaps for months. There are natural hollows, crannies and even chimneys common in this type of stone and some of these imperfections appear to be emphasized — perhaps to the point of influencing the selection process.

A receiving socket in the circle was prepared and the stone was rolled into position as a short ramp was cut into the wall of the waiting pit. Yoked with outriggers, the slab had a large weight fastened near the top on skids as twin tree trunks were stationed vertically outside. From the crossbar of this trestle, rope was bound to the timbered stone. Directed by workers, a team of oxen then pulled the ropes until it was lifted high enough for the counterweight to slide, tipping the mass down the ramp and into the hole.

Having done the lion's share of work, counterweight and skids were removed as the precise task of righting and seating the stone was completed. No doubt stoutly braced, it was backfilled with packing stones, chalk rubble and even a few tools.

The above describes, more or less, the most realistic process of how the stones were raised, accepted by the largest balance of researchers. The following theory was considered by two members of the team and myself as the three of us stood in the center of the monument. It illustrates with elegant simplicity how the tops were so perfectly leveled across the Circle's diameter, in addition to explaining the concept by which it might have been realized by workers acting on behalf of architects who would never live long enough to see it finished.

Thirty stone-holes were dug at the same time, then all but a few filled back in. This ensured that placement would follow design as decades rolled on, with those who envisioned it long dead. The delivered stones were shaped as detailed, but the tops were left incomplete. From either side of the Entrance they proceeded around the Circle in tandem, perhaps two stones at a time. When several were situated, the desired height was scribed onto one on the west side, which was then leveled across to the opposing stone. *(The west side of the henge is slightly higher than the east and would have been used as the benchmark. I specifically suspect Stone-23.)*

Workers then sculpted the stone down to the scribe-line, with tenons shaped into the saddle as they proceeded. Consistent spacing between survivors tend to suggest that a common measure was used to position them, such as a stout stick or perhaps merely a simple length of string. Today, on those stones with missing lintels, every one of the now weather-worn bulbs are easily seen extruding up from those level tables.

Repeat this process until a few of the stones are installed, then lintels could be fashioned and set. The uprights would have had the distance between adjacent stones tenons measured, with the mass-produced lintels then fitted with appropriately spaced mortises. Unlike regular soil, chalk is extremely dense and stable, so very little compression occurs when acted upon by mass. This means that, as soon as the sculpting on the upright was complete, the lintel could be seated without delay.

A trestle was centered between the two stones, straddling them inside and out, whereby the six-ton lintel could be hoisted and its mortises fitted onto the opposing tenons, capping the arrangement at nearly 16 feet. I have little doubt this procedure took less than a day. The final smoothing could then be applied to the interior at any time afterward. We know the sarsens were finished in their final position rather than when prone because the polish is only executed to about eight feet, or the distance a person can comfortably reach from a step-stool.

CIRCLE STONES

The considerable number of subtle features in the Sarsen Circle are perhaps even more impressive than its shape or size. About one hundred feet in diameter, the circumference is nearly perfect while the stones' placements are symmetrical across its radial, meaning each stone is opposed by another across the center, rather than by a vacancy. As discussed, the pits in which they stand were likely all dug at the same time and filled in to mark positions while awaiting an occupant — leaving no possibility for guesswork by future generations.

Was the Circle ever completed? With the 2013 discovery of the parchmarks for missing stones -17 and -18 I decided it must have been. But upon examining the Circle in person, it could turn out to be otherwise.

After the thirty pits were scoured out, stones were eventually planted in them, a process taking perhaps 100 years. But the quality of them falls off sharply as we proceed around to the southwest, past S-23 in the west and S-11 in the south. The exception is with robust Stone-16 and presumably -15. These straddle the winter solstice axis — a key position — so along with the Entrance Stones, were no doubt erected during the initial period.

Therefore, as there is strong supposition for every other contiguous stone in the ring, perhaps -17 and -18 were never raised. Did the vaunted builders of Stonehenge simply get bored and eventually wander off? The strongest argument against this is the Avenue, which we know was built long after the Circle. This tends to infer that the monument's main function remained relevant for centuries, so why would they leave it incomplete?

———————————————— • ————————————————

LEFT: *Stone-23 of the northwest Circle from the interior. Considered stable, -23 was never adjusted — surprising all when it collapsed in 1963! It turns out this stone was stoutly bumped in 1958 when neighbor S-22 was cleared. Re-erected the next year, it's the last stone to be worked.*

RIGHT: *Stone-10 of the south quadrant is a fine example of the tapering each stone underwent during the shaping process. Though the lintels are long gone, two tenons remain on its upper saddle, indicating that there were capstones slung between it and undersized Stone-11.*

BELOW: *Though once as tall as all the others, slim and outward-leaning Stone-11 is missing its top third. It was purposely installed as the smallest member of the Circle.*

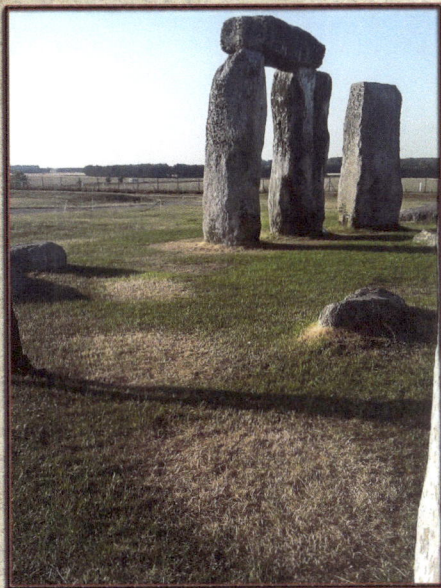

The blistering heat of July 2013 revealed the previously undetected parchmarks for Stones -17 and -18, seen as the two in the foreground. Was the Circle actually completed?

'Pregnant' Stone-16 on the south west axis. At winter solstice her bounty is proudly displayed to the dying sun; she will deliver new life at vernal equinox.

ABOVE: *Stone-3 in the east quadrant. An aspect on many stones is the hollows, pits, and crannies. Because they were first bonded in shallow swamp, we're seeing the impressions of roots and fallen palm trees.*

TOP: *Stones -21, -22, and -23 on the west side. Stone-23 is an example of fine craftsmanship, even as its neighbors are less well-fashioned.*

MIDDLE: *A blustery squall races over the timeless ruin.*

LEFT: *Stone-28 and his wife scowled as I passed — yet another ephemeral intruder into their eternal solitude.*

It's often said that -28 has a face carved into it, with eyes, nose and brow. Is this just what we want to see? Maybe, but there's also tooling marks on it which suggest an effort to amplify a few uncanny natural features.

Sorry, Stonehenge enthusiasts — there's no way to break it to you other than with the truth. Though fallen Stones -12 and -14 have taken a beating over the years, enough of them remain to tell us that they're *not* the most beautiful examples.

It's been determined that the Circle was only intended to be seen publically from the Entrance, so despite the possibility of it being incomplete, much less effort was made in crafting the rear uprights.

LEFT: *Seen from the bottom, Stone-12 has fallen outward from the Circle.*

BELOW: *Stone-12 shown from its top.*

ABOVE: In the 1680s John Aubrey said of Stone-14: "*One of the great Stones that lies downe, on the west side, hath a cavity something resembling the print of a mans foot; concerning which, the Shepherds and countrey people have a Tradition (which many of them doe stedfastly believe) that when Merlin conveyed these Stones from Ireland by Art Magick, the Devill hitt him in the heele with that stone, and so left the print there.*"

BELOW: *Stone-14 has fallen inward from the Circle. Though the initial collapse is not recorded, it didn't hit the ground right away. Over the last few centuries artwork and early photographs show its incremental decline before becoming fully prone about a hundred and twenty years ago. It now rests on Bluestone-38.*

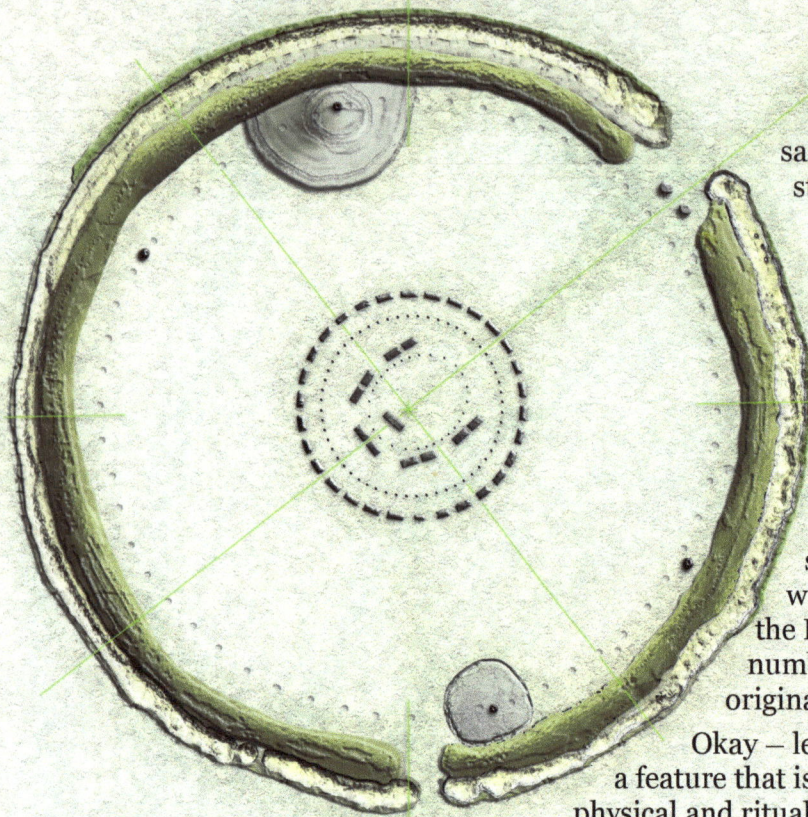

There's little doubt about the timeline here. Stonehenge went from a full set of sarsens with *no* bluestones to a full set *with* bluestones. But how were they arranged in between?

It seems the builders were never pleased with how the small ones should look before settling on a keep-it-simple motif, which maintained an inveterate elegance. Our arguments begin when we discuss how many stones there were in the two settings, or even how they looked.

Numbers for the outer set vary from more than 65 to as few as 40. Inner set discussions usually hinge on not only the number, but the shape. In review of what's known, most agree it was originally an oval, reduced to a horseshoe by the Romans or perhaps others long in the past. The number of edited stones is thought to be 19, with an original total of 26 or 27.

Okay — let's roll the clock back a moment and talk about a feature that isn't at the site, but which has great influence on physical and ritual aspects at Stonehenge. Flip back to Mr Dunn's map on page ten and follow the sweep of the Avenue over to the shores of the Avon, on the right. Here we see 'Bluestonehenge'. Well before the time in *this* picture, that location was where ritual cremations took place for subsequent interment in the Aubreys at the big site. It appears to have been in operation for quite some time.

In spite of confusion on the mid-term arrangements, it's known with a certain degree of confidence roughly how many bluestones were originally obtained from Preselli. When the crescent and double circle were first erected around the Trilithons it appears that there were up to thirty bluestones unaccounted for. Were they stacked up off to the side? Most unlikely. When the West Amesbury Henge, the actual name of the riverside feature, was discovered in 2008, it was found to include a setting of about twenty-eight bluestones, the age of which predate both its own henge and the Avenue itself. Coinciding more or less with the original installation of the bluestone crescent and circle at the Citadel, it's assumed that the leftovers from the big site were carried down to the river to construct an oval stone palisade around the cremation facility. Mystery solved.

Based on their spacing, I believe there were fifty-six bluestones in the outer circle and twenty-eight in the inner oval. It appears the workers trotted back down to the river, retrieved the originals and rebuilt the oval within the Trilithons. Then they dug the other site's henge as a replacement. Whether or not they continued using the Aubreys for anything other than curiosities at this point, the number fifty-six remained significant. Divisible by seven, it was by then recognized as the number of days in a week. Multiply by four and we get twenty-eight, or their common month. But in saying this, evil trolls would be quick to spring from the dank cave of internet anonymity and caustically reveal that the sidereal lunar month is *not* twenty-eight days, but 29.5.

Oh dear ... my ironclad, carefully crafted theory is chucked right out the window! Thanks a lot, evil trolls!

Now count the stones in the Sarsen Circle. There's thirty and this fits nothing. Or does it? As shown, Stone-11 is quite slender, not nearly the width of the others. Also, it falls just to the east side of the south cardinal as it travels through to the Southern Causeway. So in counting the stones again we come up with twenty-nine ... and a half. This suggests there's some connection, carried from ancient times, between the S-11 position and the moon, while further reinforcing that in the Gap, the adjacent Barrow and the cardinal direction, the old belief system still played an important role — even though Sun and Stone had become premiere.

Moving on, we see another addition to the complex in the form of a little henge surrounding the Heelstone. What's interesting here is it appears the fill was cast into the interior of the ring, and so it has no bank inside or out. This is either because the stone had been in place for centuries, or the builders foresaw the Avenue.

Yet another asterisk on the long list of questions we'll never have answers for.

Here we have Peter Dunn's interpretation of the West Amesbury Henge in its heyday. Brought down river by boat from the Durrington Walls settlement, the mortal remains of a notable chieftain are delivered with solemn ceremony to the cremation facility. Seen to the right rear is a great throng of people waiting to witness the proceedings, patiently standing where the Avenue will one day terminate. Unseen from here, a mile beyond the screening ridge to the left, is where this high-status leader will arrive at Stonehenge — his final destination.

About half a mile or so to the northeast is an ancient trading and travel area called Blick Mead, located within the woodland of Vespasian's Camp. Still wreathed in many legends, it's so named as it was thought to have been the location of a villa built by the eponymous Roman Emperor. It's now known to be immensely older. Perhaps this is where the mortuary personnel lived, duly separate and apart from the mainstream population.

Officials approach the cortege to accept tokens of credential from an imposing clan representative while the former leader's oldest son stands by in royal blue awaiting the conference of authority. His mother and young sibling hover nearby. This venerated institution cements the passage of an unbroken patronomic line, while dignitaries, friends and other mourners stand at left, bearing witness to the transfer of power.

Powerful spirit-relics line the short path to the river, acting as wards against unauthorized intrusion, while a young girl and her brother look on from their covert perch in a tree. The interior of the stone palisade smolders in preparation to receive its offering as attendants at the left rear assemble a wicket onto which the remains will be placed in the fire. At the conclusion of the day-long process the host will adjourn to the Citadel where this chieftain's leather-bound ashes will be interred within a prepared and waiting Aubrey Hole.

The picture's attention to detail is remarkable and we even see tongues, grooves and tenons on a few of the Bluestones, all of which are later represented at Stonehenge.

ABOVE: *Pretty Sammy Glastonbury gestures triumphantly between Bluestones -49 and -31. The size and scale of the bluestones is routinely overlooked when compared with the big boys, but as shown here, they are not so small when seen next to such an exuberant young lady. Like the entrance stones behind her, these two are situated slightly farther apart to allow passage of the sun at either solstice.*

ABOVE: *Bluestone-42 pokes up through the turf on the northwest side of the circle.*

LEFT: *Broken Bluestone-66 was excavated in 1953. Whitened by a thousand years of below-surface moisture, the tongue running along its south side is still visible.*

LEFT: *BS-68, with the carefully incised intrusion along its west side, has long been a puzzle for researchers. Though the groove itself is unexplained, it's now known that this stone was likely part of a previous setting, either at the River Avon or somewhere in Wales before being transported to its present location.*

Nearly eight feet tall, for many years Stone-56 leaned against this finely sculpted example, which prevented its collapse. Yet, in 1901 for reasons unknown, Professor William Gowland neglected to straighten it when he righted its adjacent, world-famous neighbor.

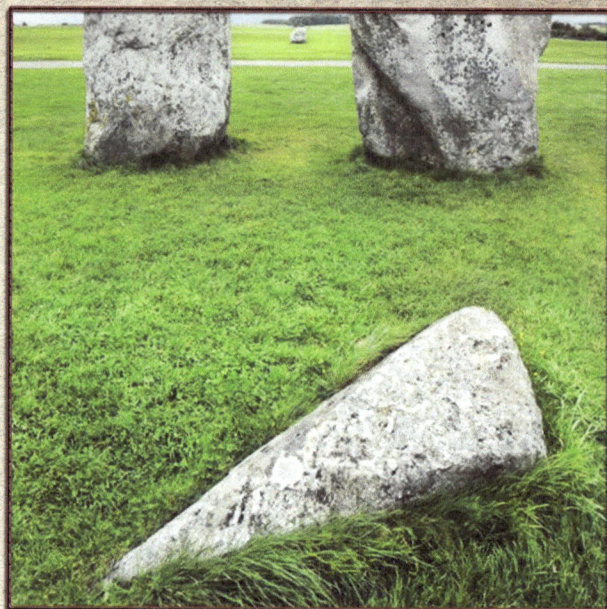

ABOVE: *BS-36 as excavated in 1953. Notice the two mortises and fine craftsmanship. Used as a lintel in a previous incarnation, it wound up as a circle stander and was returned to the hole after being examined.*

BELOW: *Humans provide scale for BS-62 and -63 between the East- and South Trilithons.*

TWO THAT GOT AWAY

Although a review of the numbered layout map is admittedly confusing, a pattern does eventually emerge with regard to the outer Bluestone ring. But allowing for stones that have fallen this way or that still leaves two stubs which wind up nowhere near the intended circle. They didn't just get up and walk away ... did they?

Shown at left above, BS-44 in the north quadrant looks to have wandered over to the feet of the North Trilithon. At right, BS-35-b in the south is tucked in right next to Stone-10, well off the ring. What's up with that? Clearly not intentionally placed, the reasoning is quite prosaic. Like most stone circles, over time Stonehenge had its share of robbers. Twenty-two lintels, a host of blues, and even five full-sized sarsens are no longer on-site.

This curiousity is further detailed a bit later in our story, but with regard to the two mentioned here, notice the direction in which they both seem to be going. Toward the nearby village of Amesbury. So I suggest robbers pulled them up and started the move when something happened to halt the process. They left the stones where they were and never came back. Busted by the land baron? Cursed by evil spirits? Called away to dinner?

Obviously we'll never know for sure, but somewhere there's a church wall or barn foundation that's missing a couple of rocks.

●

Below, Bluestone-32 huddles protectively over fallen -150. At right is elegantly sculpted Bluestone-68, with -67 at its feet.

This peculiar pile of rocks in a field is visually uncommon and quite impressive when seen up close. While there's general rumination on how they got the top ones up, often overlooked is that no other Neolithic project in the world has them, and are among the numerous reasons which make Stonehenge so unique.

ABOVE: *Lintel-101 over the entrance was surely the first to be seated. It's scribed into the saddles of the two opposing uprights for reasons unknown. Conscious of the critical symmetry, perhaps the original thickness overwhelmed the eye, or maybe all were intended to fit like this. Considering the amount of work required to craft each one, it appears that a uniform dimension is what was finally settled upon.*

ABOVE LEFT: *Peter Dunn shows how the lintels were fitted.*

LEFT: *When Stone-59 of the North Trilithon came down it shattered into three chunks. L-160 came with it and also broke in three. Being out in the middle of the court proved disastrous and today they appear as hefty lumps of rock, rounded by the ages and nearly unidentifiable as anything fashioned by hand.*

Lintel-156 of the Great Trilithon now lays across the Altar Stone. Notice the mortises and its graceful arc.

The Circle lintels are all curved inside and out, so when installed would simulate an unbroken ring around the 315-foot circumference. Additionally, all of them had lock-joints in either end to prevent any shifting. Three feet thick by 3.5 feet broad, they average 10-feet 6-inches long and each weighs about six-tons.

The Trilithon lintels are single stones set to the exterior width of the two uprights. The smallest of them is about twelve tons, while beefy -154 of the South Trilithon is a whopping seventeen tons.

Illustrating the generations it took to get them all up, the tenons of the Great Trilithon are situated outboard of its uprights, while the North's are inboard.

0 10 25   50   75   100
Scale in Feet

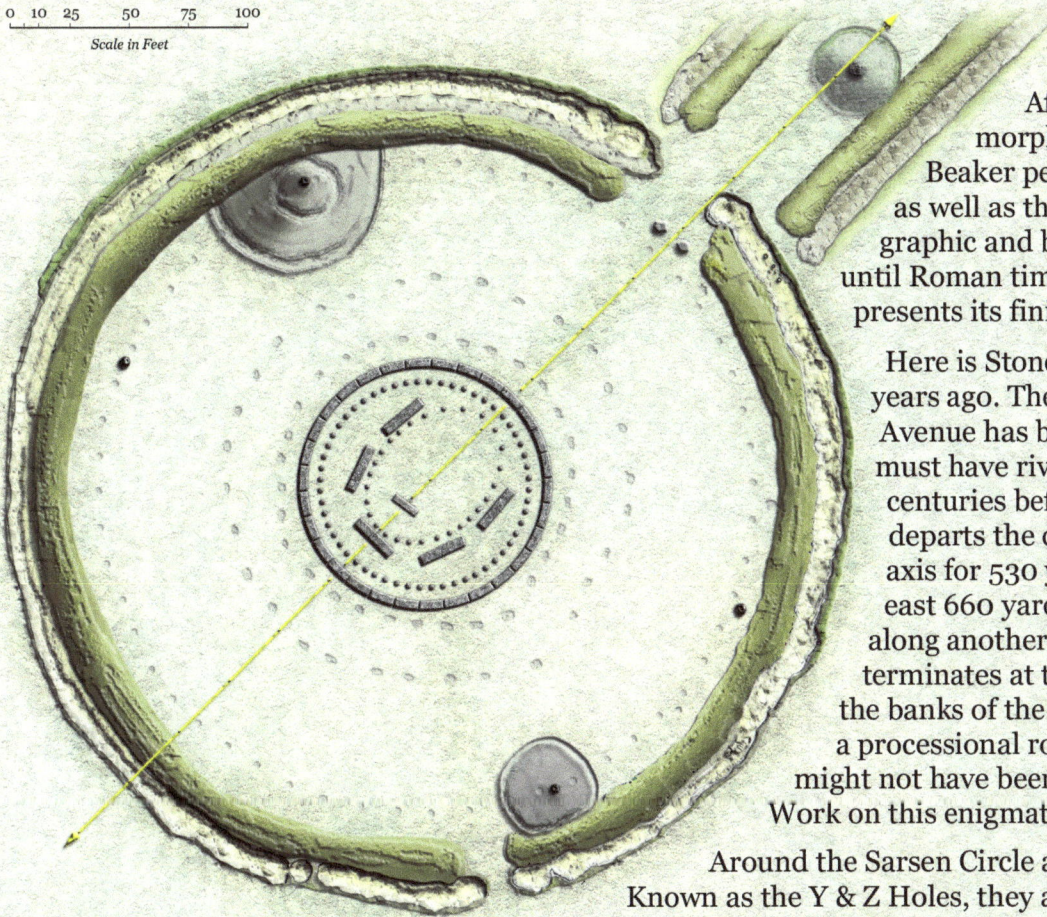

After twelve long centuries, the morphing of the Windmill Hill and Beaker people into the Wessex culture, as well as the distillation of celestial, geographic and building expertise unmatched until Roman times, the Citadel of the Cosmos presents its finished form and in full regalia.

Here is Stonehenge in its last stage, 3,600 years ago. The painstaking, labor-intensive Avenue has been completed in a work that must have rivaled the initial build so many centuries before. A mile and a half long, it departs the ditch, centered on the solstice axis for 530 yards before abruptly turning east 660 yards to a southeast curve. Then, along another straight run of 1000 yards, it terminates at the West Amesbury Henge on the banks of the River Avon. Long considered a processional route, new evidence suggests it might not have been as well trod as first thought. Work on this enigmatic aspect continues to unfold.

Around the Sarsen Circle are some intriguing elements. Known as the Y & Z Holes, they are 2 rings of 30 scours which roughly align to the stones, but whose execution was woefully performed. Sometimes seen as parchmarks, the Y & Z holes are the final additions to Stonehenge, though it's unclear what their intent might have been. More recent than the Avenue, I suspect they were dug by a Bronze Age people to whom the original purpose was forgotten. Chips of bluestone have been recovered from several, suggesting they were graves. But the two sets are separated by 100 years, so why spend perhaps three generations digging sixty graves yet put nothing in them? Were they intended for stones or trees? We will likely never know.

How Stonehenge might have looked around 2,000 years ago — old even then. All modern features have been removed in this picture, though the two nearby barrows would have existed at that time.

Peter Lorimer imagines how the Avenue appeared 4,000 years ago.

On the Stonehenge alignment.
The white dots are grazing sheep.

Traces of a distant run in the Avenue can still
be detected slashing across modern plowmarks.

The approach. Standing on the solstice alignment as an epic John Constable sky rages overhead.

In Adam Stanford's great fish-eye shot we see an elevated view of the Sarsen Circle and Trilithon set. Easy to see from this angle, each upright is slightly different in appearance, giving them individuality — some say personality, which may be more accurate in several examples.

Scale is frequently an issue when looking at the stones with nothing else in the picture for comparison, so for those who like to think in terms of dimensions, I'm here to tell you that the circle is about 100 feet in diameter, the outer stones average 13-feet out of the ground and each weighs between 21 and 22 tons. Stone-16, hidden from view to the rear, is the most robust of the Circle survivors, coming in at around 24 tons. With the lintel cap, the arrangement is just under 16 feet tall — the equivalent of standing at an upper second storey window. Each lintel is 10.5 feet long, 3.5 feet wide, 3 feet thick and weigh about 6 tons.

Laid out radially from the center, the Circle stones are positioned at 10.5 feet apart on-center — necessarily the same distance as the lintels are long. The top surface, or saddle, is half that, while the base of each averages 7-feet 10-inches. This is determined by adding 16-inches to the saddle width on either side of the centerline, which produces the stone's taper and an allowance for a 32-inch space between them, more or less. Therefore, all the ratio's of the circle design are governed by derivatives of the lintel length. Bear in mind that only the height and lintel length are essential to this formula. All others are averaged by peculiarities in the various stones, in addition to the two solstice apertures being wider than general. Precisely placed, mysterious Stone-11 was originally the same height as all the others, though its width is halved. Long debated as being ancillary, its consistent on-center position persuades us of its original intent.

As impressive as the Sarsen Circle is, it's dwarfed by the monumental Trilithons. With their lintels installed, these 3-stone arches graduate in height from 19 to 26 feet. Stone-56, the single remnant of the Great Trilithon, is seen at center-rear, and whose weight exceeds 40 tons. To its left is the South Trilithon, the most massive of all, with each of its uprights coming in at 52 tons. Its finely crafted lintel weighs 17. The U-shaped Trilithon set fits nicely into a square that's about 50-feet on a side, or half the Circle's width.

Against this backdrop of giants it's easy to overlook the deceptively diminutive bluestones, many of which are taller than a man and average four tons. A standard automobile weighs less than two. The outer circle stands about six feet inside the sarsen ring, while the inner set is positioned more tightly to the Trilithon stones. The interior members are generally taller and more elegantly shaped than those of the outer ring.

The unique execution of this integrated structure tells us that the engineering prowess of the builders was quite a bit more impressive than simply throwing up a random pile of rocks. Collectively, but in separate episodes, the stones took perhaps 125 years to erect, but the builders' cohesive template passed seamlessly through at least four generations despite the inability to draw a plan. This speaks to a unified culture with an alternative communication skill-set who transmit these sophisticated levels of construction down to the present day.

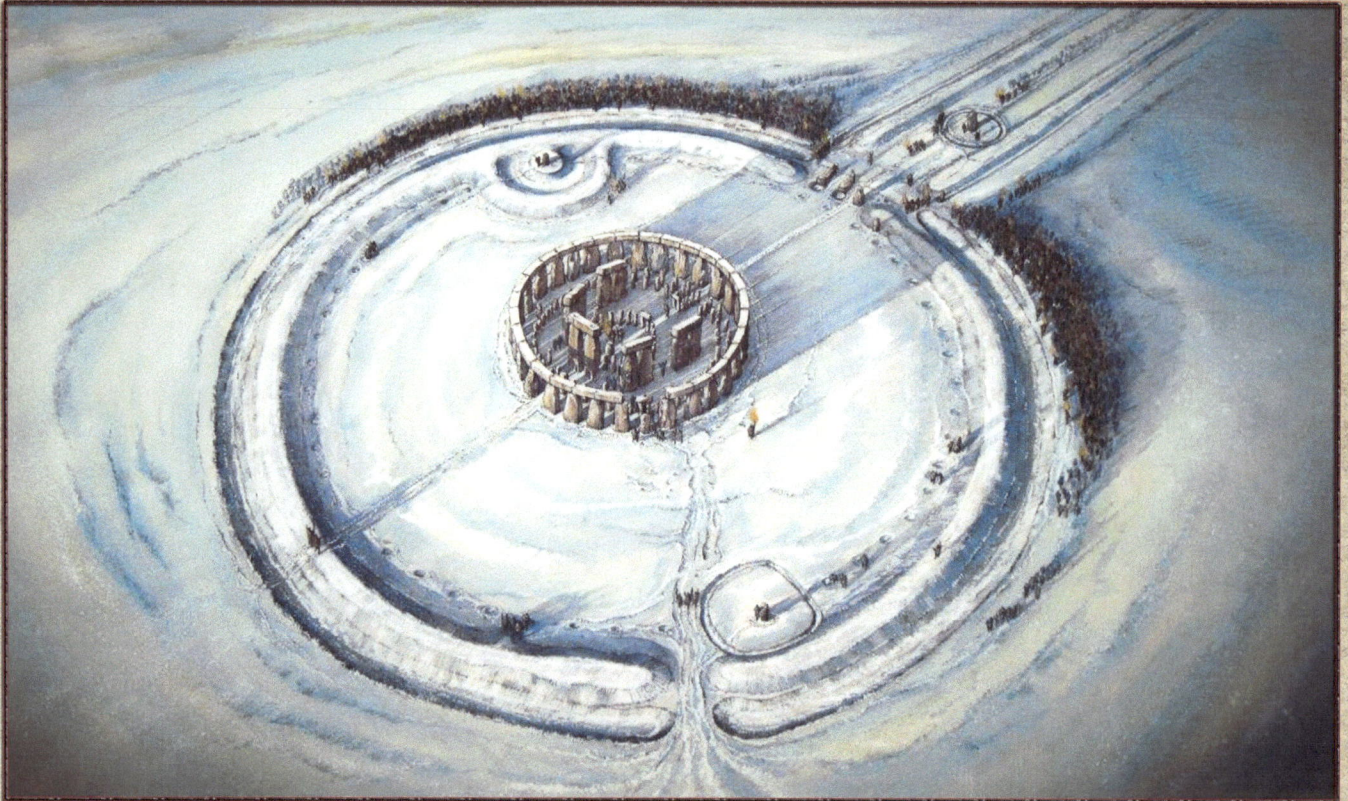

Deep within the shrouding Sarsen Circle, religious officials perform the traditional arcane rituals of the season as winter solstice Sun dips into the southwest horizon. Long dark shadows cast by the towering stones are emphasized by a blanket of new-fallen snow. The last narrow shock of sunlight races through the edifice to splash on the distant face of the rugged Solstice Stone as members of the public jostle tightly at the ditch perimeter on either side of the Avenue.

Staff and security personnel occupy various ceremonial positions around the site as the moment approaches and a hush of anticipation descends over the throng. The capricious vagaries of English weather often prevent witnessing Sun's actual appearance at the appointed time, so this year the crowds are huge and swollen with the excitement of not only being permitted so close to the fabled stones of the mystic Citadel, but with a promise of the hearty, convivial and days-long celebrations which follow.

SUMMER SOLSTICE SUNRISE   2015 CE

Long-lens pan from the Amesbury-10 Disc Barrow as a watery dawn breaks over the fabled stones.

Hippies in love on the South Barrow.

Authentic Druids and their erstwhile retinue.

Staff Meeting.

Gypsies in the palace.

From the Drove.

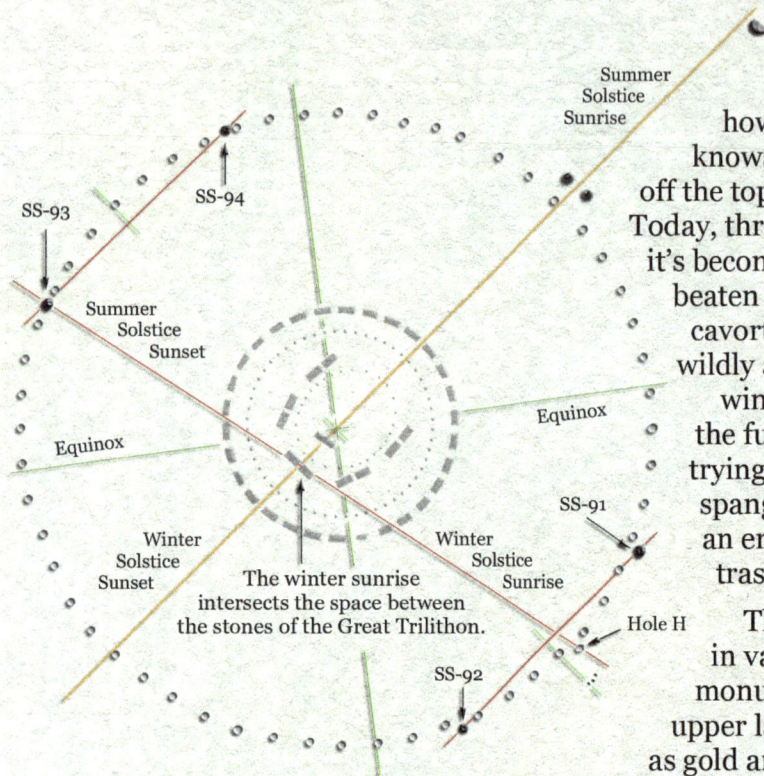

SS-93

SS-94

Summer
Solstice
Sunset

Summer
Solstice
Sunrise

Equinox

Equinox

Winter
Solstice
Sunset

Winter
Solstice
Sunrise

SS-91

The winter sunrise
intersects the space between
the stones of the Great Trilithon.

Hole H

SS-92

Well known features at Stonehenge include the ditch, Aubrey Holes and obviously its stones — and how these interact with the sun. Pretty much everyone knows about the summer solstice and how the sun peens off the top of the Heelstone as it arcs into the sky on 21 June. Today, throngs of people attend celebrations on that date and it's become a widely anticipated summer festival. Drums are beaten out of time, cymbals shrilly clang, new-age dancers cavort, solemn, mysterious ceremonies are performed by wildly anachronistic druids, and copious amounts of beer, wine and all sorts of other things are consumed. Far in the future, people will look back and scratch their heads, trying to figure out why the many thousands of colorfully spangled folks of the 20th and 21st centuries would wait an entire year to deposit their accumulated stockpiles of trash and litter at this ancient, hallowed place …

This has been going on for a couple of hundred years in various incarnations, and there's little doubt that the monument has seen such things since it was built. In the upper layers of turf are found coins from every age, as well as gold and silver jewelry, bottles, buttons, forks, knives and every imaginable item that can be lost by visitors in 2,000 years.

Yet one of the more curious things about this aspect of on-site archaeology is that, other than a few of the tools used to build it, nothing but a fistful of broken pottery has ever been recovered from original times. This tells us that it was a place set aside by the society and no one ever actually lived there.

The modern aspect can trace its roots back to the 18th century when a well-respected antiquarian spent years surveying and writing about the monument, along with the wide area surrounding it. In 1740 William Stukeley published his comprehensive tome *Stonehenge: A Temple Restor'd to the British Druids*, and it became the definitive touchstone reference for nearly a hundred years. Old Bill was so convinced that Stonehenge had been built by the druids that he eventually became one himself. The frontispiece of his remarkable, heavily illustrated book shows the wonderful woodcut of *A British Druid*, now known to be a portrait of him.

Unfortunately, the earliest, wholly second-hand reference we have of British druids is from c.50 BCE by no less than Julius Caesar, though his accounts are surely biased against the mysterious forest dwellers. Even generously allowing them plenty of time to become culturally invested — say around 400 years — still leaves us with 15 centuries where they simply could not have been extant, the passage of oral tradition notwithstanding.

In terms of sun celebrations, one of the things that has recently come to light is that, while it's virtually certain that the summer event was observed, the opposing winter event was most likely far more important to the ancient people in the scheme of things.

By the time the solar apex arrives in June, everything has become warm and green. Fish jump, lambs gambol, crops begin to grow and the days have gotten long. But at winter solstice all has become bleak, cold and dreary. The days have become very short while warmth and light seem to have fled the land. Many centuries before, this has been a fearful time. *Will Sun ever return?* The Citadel was built, in part, to highlight assurance.

As we know, the Great Trilithon was finely finished on all sides — not just on the interior. Also, although the quality of the Circle stones fall off toward the southwest, Stone-16, on the axis, is big and heavily worked. Presumably Stone-15 was too. If we were to stand in the center of the monument at sunset on 21 December, we'd have seen the sun descend to the horizon right into the slender slot between the huge stones of the Great Trilithon. It still does this. It's likely that some form of observance was conducted in this rear area.

We know that feasts were held at this time, with people coming from far and wide bringing goods and livestock with them — certainly from Scotland and probably the continent. They came to bid Sun farewell, and we've learned there's some compelling evidence in the surrounding area which speaks to this.

In researching information for pages you haven't seen yet, I made a discovery concerning a certain curiosity that should be highlighted. It not only helps solve the Aubrey Hole problem, but casts light on the forethought of the builders, demonstrating that though the moon was the design criteria in the beginning, the sun and what was thought to be correct cardinals, were important enough to include as well.

The drawing on the right shows in green lines both the summer and winter solstice alignments, in addition to their opposing equatorial counter-parts. Each set is composed of numerous parallel lines, the central of which has three points of contact — that is: two Aubreys and the center. Other than the cardinals shown below, no other combination of meridians do this, strongly inferring it was intentional. Important to bear in mind is that these alignments do *not* work today, as the sunline has shifted a degree and a half east.

The solution to another mystery is revealed when we notice that all three lettered holes are also included, in addition to those three peculiar postholes on the bank to the southeast. The holes -F, -G and -H, as well as the postholes, were discovered in the 1920s and were thought to be connected in some way to the Aubreys. But they are slightly outside the ring and don't share the same characteristics. The three postholes are on the bank's crest and align with the then-solstice. The upper of them serves to anchor the central equatorial opposition.

Below we see the alignments created by the cardinal directions. Referring back to page 17 we'll remember that these directions were poorly calculated, with North/South sighted when the star Thuban was west of true, and East/West sighted from the center of the henge to incorrect points on either horizon. But this didn't stop our plucky builders, and they positioned the Aubreys on those erroneous nodes anyway. The process was the same as the solar alignments: the middle meridian makes three points of contact, with the parallels following suit.

The red lines are the exception to this rule, in that the anchor for them does not cross the center or an Aubrey. This is because it's the winter solstice sunrise and the opposing summer solstice sunset. It originates at pesky Hole-H and travels over to the Station Stone-93 position, most likely marked by a post in the early days.

Another curiosity is we see this line crossing directly between the two uprights of the future Great Trilithon, and makes the positioning of this imposing stone arch easier to understand. Notice that the Altar Stone is also cocked at this angle, while maybe a couple of Bluestones were too. Some of these alignments are perfect and some are so close they're shown. Others may have been intended, but I'm the guy sitting in front of a 40-inch monitor drawing lines in Photoshop, warm with a nice cup of coffee at my elbow. I'm *not* one of the the guys standing out on the blustery Salisbury Plain using tall sticks and sharp eye attempting to align hole positions across a 300-foot diameter. There's bound to be a few mistakes. Important to keep in mind: those folks didn't have the benefit of seeing any of these things from above like we do on a map or aerial photograph. They no doubt thought their circles were round and their holes aligned just right. But even with a lack of technology and adding inevitable human error, it's still an amazing job. Saying all this begs the question ... *why did they do it?*

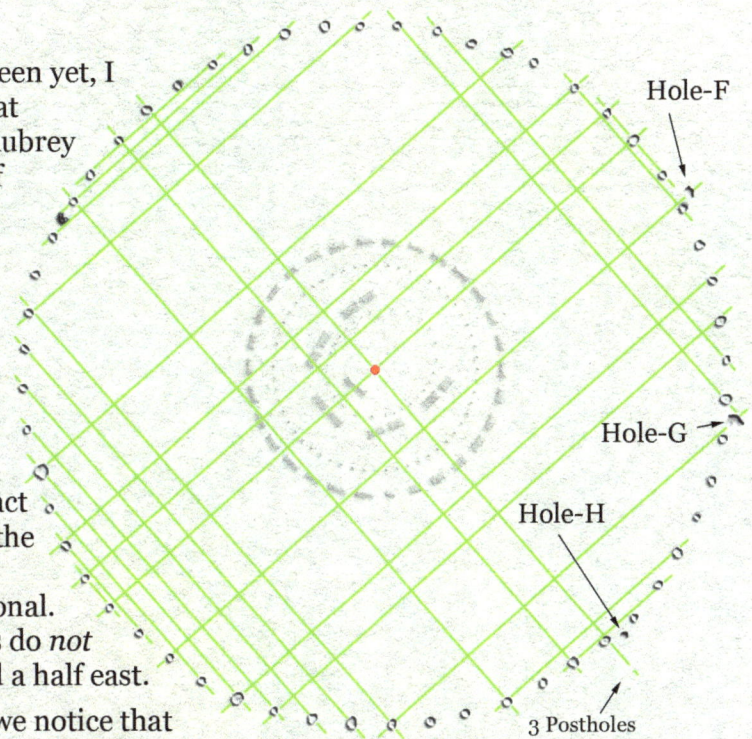

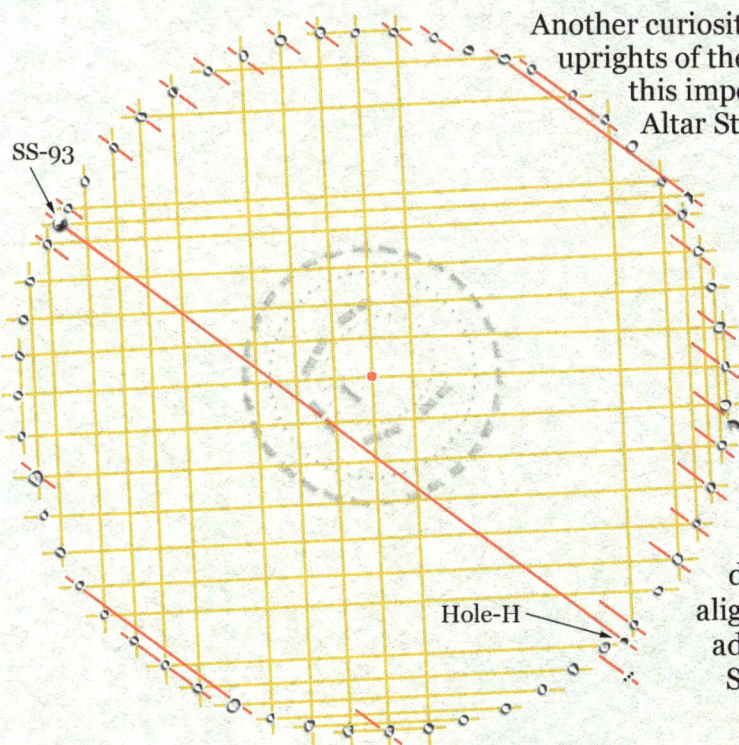

Hole-F

Hole-G

Hole-H

3 Postholes

SS-93

Hole-H

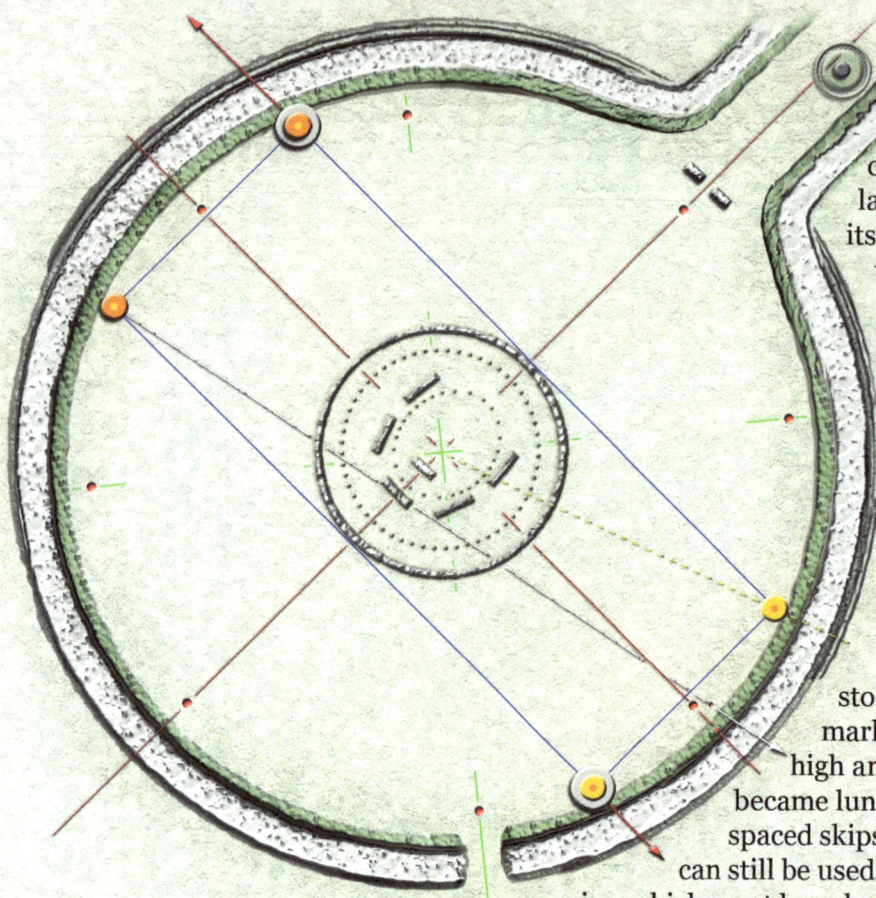

So here's what I think about all this. The stylized rendering illustrates that if the early designers had been a bit more conscientious with their references, and if the later builders could have made the sun behave itself relative to obliquity, this would have been their intent. With the accumulated traditions passed through scores of generations, Stonehenge became more than a lunar watchdog/ solar observatory. It had morphed into an explanation of the known world, with Sun as Father of Life, Moon as Death's odious usher, while they and everything else is on eternal orbit of Mother Earth, the fertile stage onto which all life is delivered. The builders had placed their elaborate Stone Citadel at the very center of the universe.

When Moon was influential, the henge itself stood for Mother Earth, with the Station Stones marking the Tropics of Cancer & Capricorn; both high and low solstice. (blue lines) Thus the Aubreys became lunar cycle-counters, with alternating, regularly spaced skips to accommodate the seasons. This calendar can still be used and reflects a complex, sophisticated worldview which must have been well-understood from the very beginning.

With the repositioned Heelstone, installation of the Trilithons and the Q & R arrangement, control was deftly transferred to the sun. When the Stone Circle was eventually erected, *it* became the representation of an everlasting Earth, its diameter now defined by the already existing Station Stones — while retaining their definition of solar/ lunar highs and lows. (Notice the Circle's diameter is the same as its distance from the bank.) Sister Moon is not brushed aside but takes a right-hand seat in the triad's pantheon. The number of Circle stones are the days it takes for her to orbit Earth, with Stone-11 as the leftover half day of the month. *The cosmic family, all under one roof!*

From the center, the yellow dashed line drawn to any Station Stone is 22.5° off the equator, or the axial tilt of the planet at that time. *Copernicus who?* The white line indicates the winter solstice sunrise as seen from SS-93, intersecting the axis between the stones of the Great Trilithon before passing through mysterious Hole-H — which means the alignment had been celebrated from the very earliest days. This is proved by the sightline being obscured by four later stones, indicating it had been situated long before those stones existed. It also infers that the Great Trilithon itself was positioned specifically to accommodate this sightline. *You just can't make this stuff up!*

The two barrows represented Sister Moon at her high and low occurrence of standstill every 9.3 and 18.6 years, (red lines). The five Trilithons, each with an alternate male/female upright, were the womb of Earth Mother. In June the Sun Father passed into the circle to make visit upon his beautiful wife, and this act ensured life's continuity throughout the universe. The Counterscarp hoodie prevented his overwhelming radiance from blessing the unworthy dead of the outer realm. Surrounded by 28 stones of the Life Egg bearing witness to this energetic rite, the recumbent Altar Stone is likely where Father's visit was mimicked by eager humans. *Hard stone. Blankets recommended!*

The rear area between the Great Trilithon and the southwest Stone Circle is where Father was bidden farewell in December. We can't know if S-15 represented a male, but bulging Stone-16 is clearly symbolic of a pregnant Earth Wife proudly displaying second-trimester bounty to dying Sun as he dipped into the uttermost depths of winter. Luckily, after three days of no apparent motion along the horizon, he rose from death to begin his northward journey once more. It's a time of excitement, celebration and feasting in anticipation of Mother's blessèd issue coming forth to usher a rebirth of the cosmos at vernal equinox, nine months after Father's conjugal solstice visit.

The Romans called their spring festival: *Saturnalia*, which was so auspicious they named a planet for it. Though quite late in the running, Christians soon tailored the zodiac-based, moon-governed vernal equinox rite to fit their new-fangled monotheism. They call it: *Easter*, where new life arrives in the world after laying dead for three days.

Here we see Stonehenge represented as a construct in both the physical and metaphoric landscape. Notice how all the previously existing features are cleverly incorporated into the matrix of concepts — Station Stones, Aubreys, and Barrows. In short, it is the entire known cosmos, with every major feature in it on orbit around Mother Earth.

Remember: this earth-centric idea was accepted as cold hard truth by almost every culture in history, finally disproved only by the work of Galileo Galilei a scant four hundred years ago. As we learned, Earth is not only round, but also a globe, and while it's a stretch to assign the knowledge of longitude to the builders of Stonehenge, (no clocks), latitude is certainly not. With proof at Avebury, their complete understanding of Sky is responsible for this.

Looking into the night, we see the velvety black rotunda dotted with points of light. While closer than the blackness, they are still very far away. The Aubreys represent those stars, and the Ancients were interred among them as wise overseers, whose purpose it was to intercede with Moon and Sun on behalf of humans. Their deeds in life were characterized by the band of twelve star-pictures through which all but Moon are locked in Sky.

Diagram labels: Source of Knowledge · Blackness beyond the Stars · Processional of the Sun King in summer · Midnight on 21 June · Most Northerly Moonset · Equator · High Orbit · 56 Stars against the Barrier · Midnight on 21 December · Life from the East / Southern England · Noon on 21 June · Death to the West · Low Orbit · Protective Barrier of the Cosmos · Noon on 21 December · Most Southerly Moonrise · 51° North Latitude · The Overworld. *Ruled by Father Sun* · Equator · Sun King in winter · The Outerworld. *Ruled by Sister Moon* · Exit to Afterlife

Beyond this blackness is where the unworthy dead resided, forever prevented from re-entering the world by the essential barrier between light and dark. The unique inner embankment was this barrier, beyond which was the endless gulf of the Eternal Empty, sole dominion of Sister Moon. Represented by the ditch, kind humans have left a few tools within it so these pitiful wretches might dig their own graves. But this thoughtful kindness had a limit, in that powerful guardians, in the form of auroch skull-relics, flanked the Southern Causeway. These fearsome spirits prevented the blind and wandering dead from re-entering the warmly lit overworld of Sun.

Earth Mother is solid and imperishable; her diameter determined by Sun and Moon. These two bodies are the same size, though Moon is closer, horribly stained and disfigured by proximity to her brilliant older brother. No doubt by scheming intention, her elaborate path periodically crosses his and on those occasions a resentful, capricious Moon attempts to wrest control of the living world, bringing darkness and death to dwell among the people. Thus far she has been defeated — driven off by the frantic exhortations to Sun by terrorized humans.

The equator/axis also played a role in the orbit of the two satellites, and this is demonstrated by how it hosts both at key times of the year. From the equator to cardinal east is 51° — Stonehenge's actual latitude — and indicated that the source of life radiated out from southern England, as ordained by Father Sun.

Another peculiarity is that only at this latitude can solstice and its equator occur in perpendicular positions. A few tens of miles north or south and the rectangle formed by the Station Stones becomes a parallelogram. There is an older henge-like structure in north Germany called Gosek which shares the same aspect, while the far later Native American medicine wheels of western Canada also display it.

Because it exists at the upper limit of the restriction, Avebury cannot have been built with the same rationale as its more specifically encoded younger sister. Though its older purpose was more celestially inclusive, and while the two remarkable stone monuments surely complemented each other in some way, perhaps this 51-degree rule hadn't been discovered at the time construction was finalized at the enormous northern complex.

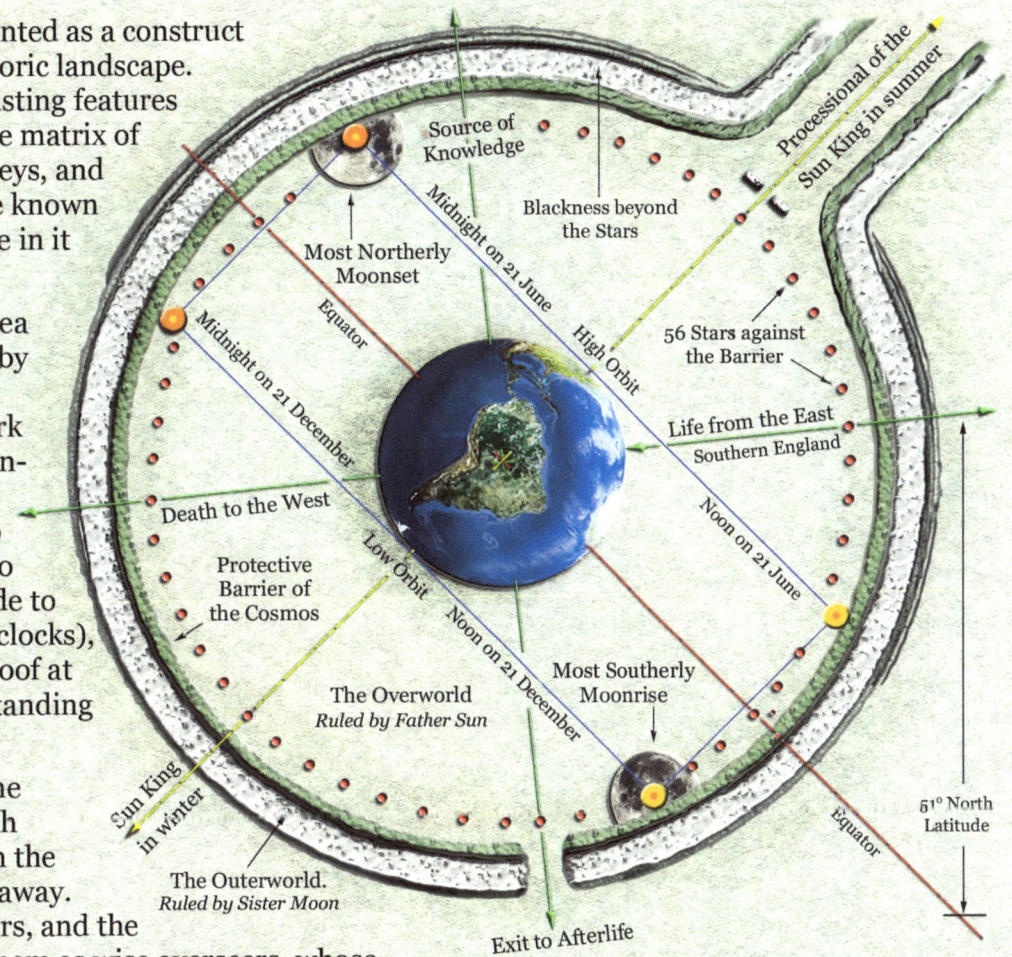

We've seen the monument progress from a simple regional graveyard designed for and overseen by Moon, on to an extraordinary edifice which had been repurposed from the relics of old, its function now shared with Sun and Earth. We know it was visited by folks from far and wide — but what if that influence ran far deeper? What if it was venerated by both the mighty and meek from distant lands who would never see it? These ancients would have known it only as the legendary thread by which their culture was bound for scores of generations. How many people have seen the Pyramids? Relatively few compared to the number who know they exist.

Now let's see if there's any, more tangible aspects of this pesky *Cosmos* concept that come into play.

North of mainland Scotland, on the rugged Orkney Islands, there's a Neolithic village called Skara Brae. Nearby is a slender isthmus flanked by two monuments known as the Stones of Stennes and the Ring of Brodgar. Set into the narrow stripe of ground between them is a complex of structures named the Ness of Brodgar. With stacked stone walls and thick turf roofs it was a hardy enclave against that capricious North Sea environment. Being excavated as we speak, this elaborate warren has winding corridors which connect the various compartments. Among many notable things about the place is there are chambers within which are neither dwelling spaces nor workshops. So indulge me: was Brodgar a kind of temple-village reserved for study or instruction?

South, across the English Channel on the lower coast of Brittany, there's a place called Carnac. This was a huge tract of land with several sets of over three thousand standing stones culled from local quarries throughout the Neolithic. Consisting of parallel rows of undressed orthostats, it's been extensively robbed over time so only seven hundred survive, but beyond conjecture there's no solid theory on what the purpose might have been.

Not far west of Wales, across another strait of water, is Ireland, which boasts a great number of monuments. Among the most impressive is a place called Newgrange, a significant passage tomb. The long corridor into it aligns with the winter solstice sunrise, and that beam is cast through an open rectangular lightbox set above the entrance where it tracks the rear wall of the passage for seven minutes on a few mornings around that date.

Of course everyone has monuments and some are almost as remarkable as that annoying pile of rocks out on the Salisbury Plain. Well, let's review what's been learned so far. The Ness of Brodgar is 3° west longitude. Within about four miles, so is Carnac. While Stonehenge is not on the same meridian, if you shoot along the setting solstice sunline for 262 miles, you hit Newgrange right on the button. The only way this could have been achieved is with a full understanding of latitude and stellar cartography. East becomes the source of life; north is the seat of knowledge or wisdom. South is where the highborn from across the region are memorialized; west is where their bodies are buried. So, while a metaphysical Stonehenge represented the center of the cosmos, its true cultural authority radiated from the heart of an international swath of real estate which comprised the entire age-long realm.

Trading throughout this region is documented in both the Neolithic and Bronze Age, while copper and the principals of agriculture had come from Europe in the first place. People from Scotland used the same pottery and house styles as those in the south and are known to have brought livestock to Durrington Walls for the solstice festivities. Newgrange was designed in part as a royal tomb — its mysterious spiral art carved to showcase Sun's growing and shrinking passage through the seasons. Call me crazy, but I believe it all connects.

RIGHT: *A north/south meridian connects the Ness of Brodgar to Carnac, with a 4-mile variation over 792 miles. The sunlines from Stonehenge intersect Newgrange, with no variation over 262 miles.*

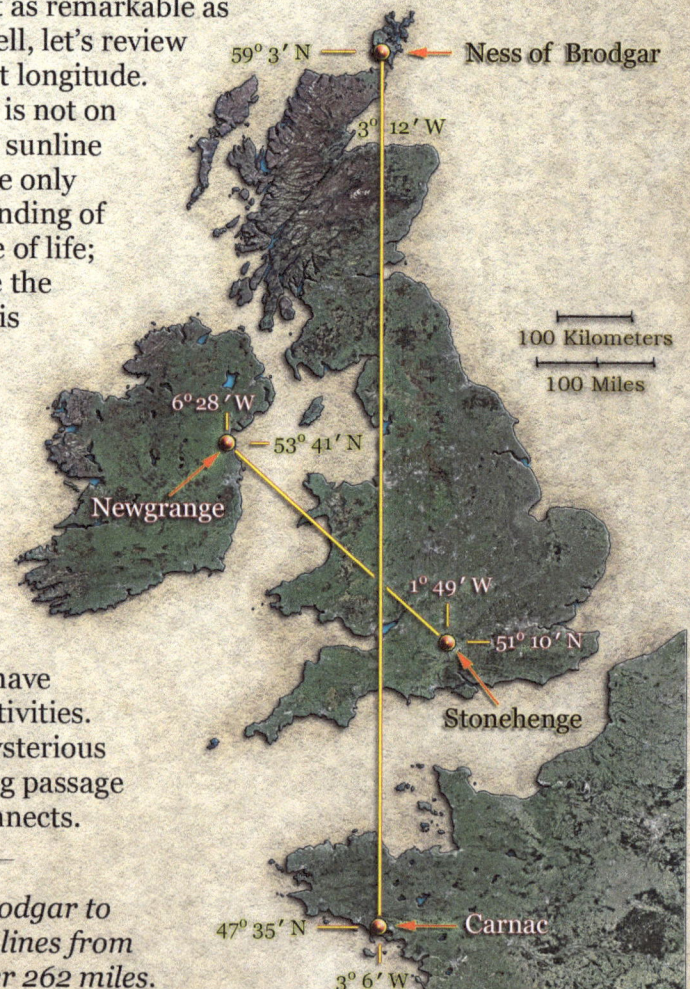

59° 3′ N — Ness of Brodgar
3° 12′ W

100 Kilometers
100 Miles

6° 28′ W
— 53° 41′ N
Newgrange

1° 49′ W
— 51° 10′ N
Stonehenge

47° 35′ N — Carnac
3° 6′ W

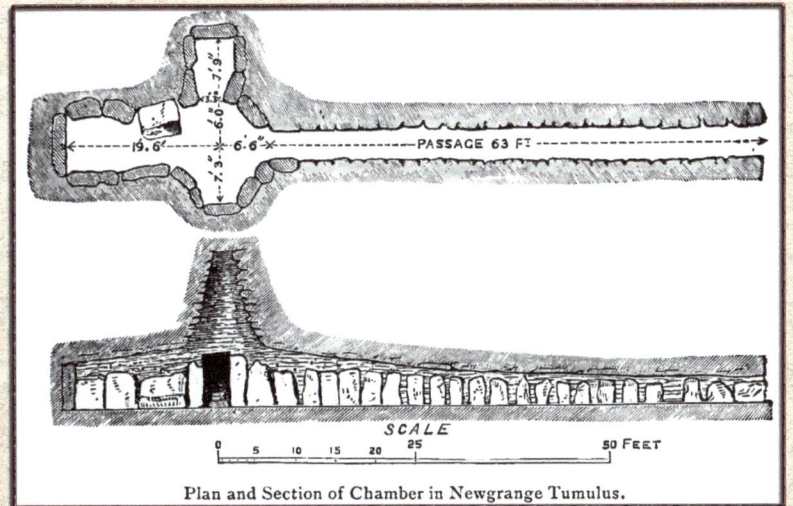

Plan and Section of Chamber in Newgrange Tumulus.

Recently the mental picture we had of Neolithic people was of brutish cave dwellers who dragged women around by the hair while yelling Yabba Dabba Doo a lot. This caricature assists in elevating the wonder we experience when witnessing the monuments they left behind, as it's even more baffling when we assign a certain wholesale ignorance to the troglodytes who built them. We now know that nothing could be further from the truth.

Let's inspect the context in which western culture evolved. The map on the following page includes Europe and the Middle East. The bull's-eye in central Iraq has ever-larger circles radiating from it which represent time, or how long it took advancements to move out from the hub. Keep in mind that this exercise is imperfect and there's some big exceptions, but generally they had developed writing, bronze and coinage in Nineveh while the savages of northern Europe were still ripping the hides from animals to keep warm while yelling Yabba Dabba Doo a lot.

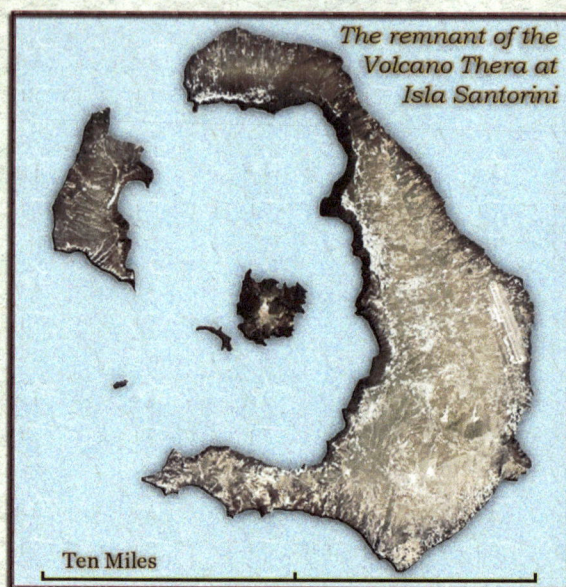

The remnant of the Volcano Thera at Isla Santorini

Ten Miles

But cultural innovation is not always measured by technology, and time spent in one location often lends itself to a pattern of growth that may equal or exceed that of other places. Western people were not on par with the east in many ways, true, but based on what we know they had developed long-standing settlements, agriculture, cloth, trade, caste systems, a kind of science/religion, arithmetic, astronomy, communication over long distance and so on which tell us their way of life was little different from their more sophisticated neighbors, or really, us. They got up each morning, went to work, got married, had kids, attended church as well as four national and many regional holidays during the year.

They had statement monuments for which our equivalents include the Eiffel Tower, Mt Rushmore or the Taj Mahal. Avebury, Carnac, Newgrange and Stonehenge are only four instances that broadcast ideas other than the permanence of death. These structures are all older than any pyramid. There was no writing, but they *did* pass their knowledge along. My idea is they sang ritual songs which survived intact for long periods, telling subsequent generations how things were to be done. With this method the Neolithic Europeans had a dandy system of dispatch which propelled their culture onward. This practice continued until around 1,600 BCE.

Then it all stopped.

Four thousand years of social, cultural and technological mobility ceased in the blink of an eye and the consequences of it erased almost every aspect of their history, aspiration and inspiration. The next we hear of Britain and its people is about 1,500 years later when those pesky Romans attempted an invasion. That didn't work out too well for them until a century or so afterward, but they nevertheless report a race of savage tribes living amid some marvelous ruins. In 50 BCE, Diodorus Siculus, a fawning Caesarian shill but otherwise noted Roman correspondent, had a late-breaking newsflash with regard to the remote, barbarous Island of the Hyperboreans:

> *The following legend is told concerning it: Leto was born on this island, and for that reason Apollo is honored among them above all other gods; and the inhabitants are looked upon as priests of Apollo after a manner, since daily they praise this god continuously in song and honor him exceedingly. And there is also on the island both a magnificent sacred precinct of Apollo and a notable temple which is adorned with votive offerings and is* circular* *in shape.*

Pretty tantalizing stuff, but was he talking about Stonehenge? Does it matter? The key is he was referring to old tales of a lapsed people who had once worshipped the sun and had impressive temples within which to do so.

At Isla Santorini in the Aegean Sea in 1,628 BCE, the volcano Thera exploded with such force and released so much ash into the atmosphere that it blotted out the sun for five years. There's evidence that volatile Mt. Hekla in Iceland erupted at nearly the same time, perhaps extending the catastrophic dark age. Dates for this double-whammy appear in trees rings from Canada, Europe and the Balkans. Another barometer for the after-effects is that all megalithic building in northwest Europe abruptly ceased. In a culture dependent upon the sun for life and belief, any survivors of mass starvation would have given this age-old paradigm a fundamental re-think.

Everything they knew, believed, reasoned or dreamed under the sun was gone in a twinkle, while the accumulated knowledge and virtually all record of their history over the millennia was forever lost to the ages.

*Some translations say: *Spherical.*

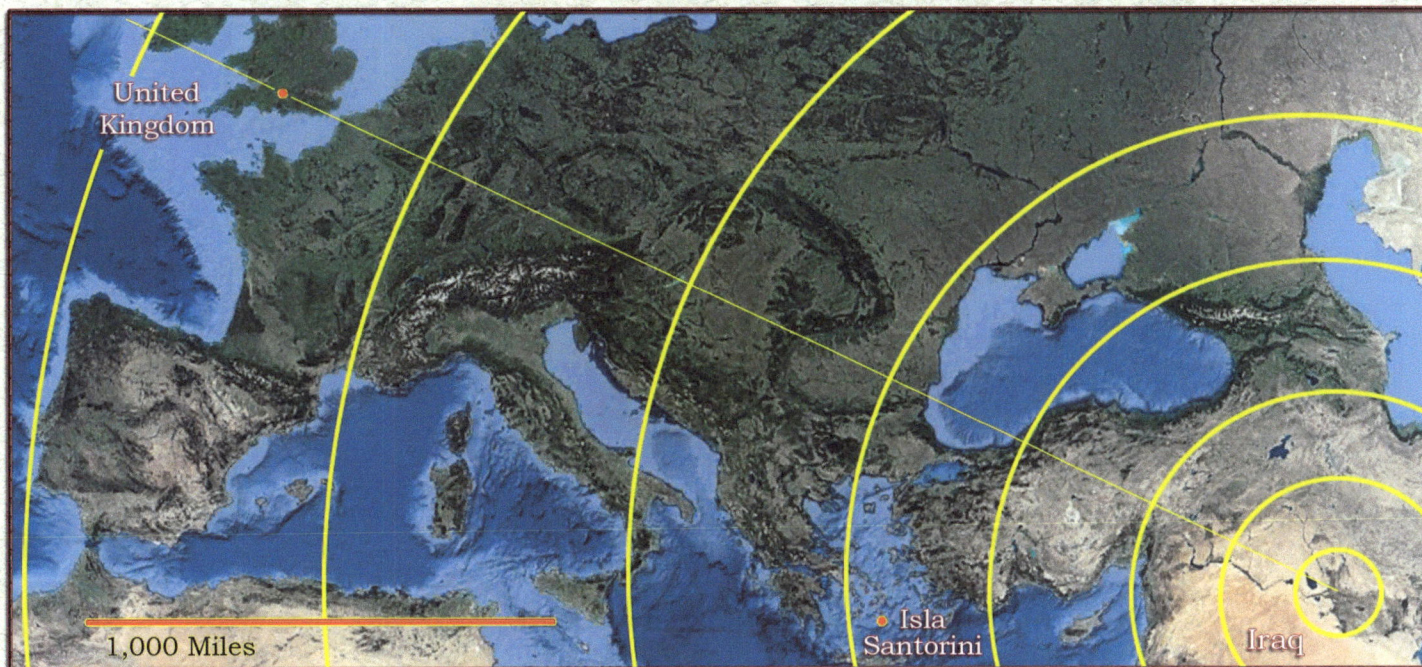

1,000 Miles

United Kingdom

Isla Santorini

Iraq

Modern humans had lived throughout the area shown here — and far beyond — for many scores of millennia, living in family and clan groups which roved far and wide following the seasonal migration of game. They began to settle in Mesopotamia, where farming was eventually developed. From these communities other sophisticated ideas radiated out, and technologies were adapted to existing traditions. After England became an island, the process there slowed considerably, so the wheel, farming, writing and metal came much later.

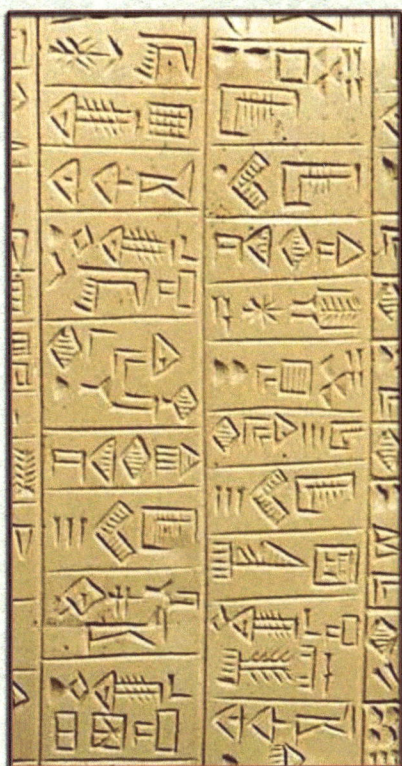

LEFT: *Sumerian mud tablet, c.4,500 years old. Read left-to-right, archaic cuneiform is among the earliest stylized writing systems and was essentially developed to keep daily or weekly records of goods usage, though detailed histories are also written in it.*

RIGHT: *The famous Bush Barrow Lozenge, recovered in 1808 less than a mile from Stonehenge. It's a sun symbol worn on the breast of a high-status male and is roughly contemporary with the tablet at left.*

"Writing has the ability to put agreements, laws and commandments on record. It made the growth of states possible. It made a continuous historical consciousness possible. The command of the priest or king and his seal could go far beyond his sight and voice and could survive his death".

HG WELLS

51

SYMBOLISM in the STONEHENGE COMPONENTS *

A disheveled male skeleton with no grave goods was found in the north ditch and dates to the late stone period. He had been killed with three or four arrows. No doubt an ignorant blasphemer trespassed into the sacred Citadel, paid the ultimate price, and was chucked like a dog into the Eternal Empty. That'll teach 'em!

Red deer antler & auroch shoulder bone tools have been recovered from the ditch; picks and shovels left behind by those who dug it. Tools sympathetically gifted to the dead for digging their own graves.

Inner Embankment. Barrier to the Outer Darkness. Originally 8 feet high. Now so soft and peppered with breaks it can no longer prevent intrusions by the unworthy — over a million of whom visit each year.

Outer Ditch. Dark Realm of the Dead. The dominion of Sister Moon. Was 6 feet deep. Now heavily silted.

NOTE: Bluestone numbers were assigned in 1880 before much serious excavation had been done. As a result many now have letters attached to them; sockets or stumps found below the surface. There was no consideration for missing stones.

Bluestones of the outer circle begin at BS-31 and end at -49, mortised BS-150 numbered out of sequence due to its peculiarity. There was no consideration for missing stones.

The ten Trilithon stones run from S-51 through -60 with Lintels L-152 -154 -156 -158 and -160. The five giant sets are named clockwise: East- South- Great- West- and North Trilithons.

The inner Bluestone Horseshoe was numbered before it was known to have originally been an oval. These stones run from BS-61 through BS-73, without consideration for missing stones.

Though confusing, this system is still in use today. Refer to the illustration inside the front cover for more clarity.

The Summer Solstice Axis
Sun arrives to make visit upon his wife.

SS-94
Missing

SS-93
Unaltered

North Barrow
Predates the ditch.
Now nearly obliterated.

Two Entrance Stones
Also shadow-casters, only
the Slaughter Stone remains.

West Trilithon
Re-erected 1958

North Trilithon
S-59 is collapsed

Stone-16: Pregnant Earth
Mother displays her
bounty to Sun Father at
winter solstice sunset.

Great Trilithon
S-55 is collapsed

The Sarsen Circle:
Mother Earth

Altar Stone
Pitched 80° off-axis to align
with winter solstice sunrise.

East Trilithon
Unaltered

South Trilithon
Righted 1964

Trilithons: The Womb
of Mother Earth

The Southern Causeway
Exit for the dead.
Now indistinguishable
from many other breaks
in the ditch & bank.

SS-92
Missing

SS-91
Now leans
on the bank

Two cattle skulls flanked
the Southern Causeway
Previously curated, they are 300 years older
than the henge and thwarted any attempt the
dead might make in returning to Sun's Domain.

South Barrow
Built over a previous
D-shaped wooden structure.
Now badly melted.

Counterscarp Embankment
Prevented the overwhelming Solstice
light of Father Sun from blessing
the dead. Now faded into the ditch.

Three Bank Postholes
Tracked the henge's shifting equator.

Hole H
Sightline from SS-93 marks
summer sunset & winter sunrise.
Passes through the Great Trilithon.

Ageless Realm of the Dead.
Dominion of Sister Moon.
Hers is the only light the dead
are permitted to experience.
In addition to being cremation
reliquaries, the Aubrey Holes
may also have represented
stars and a clever lunar calendar.
Now Invisible

The Cosmic Overworld
Dominion of Father Sun

The Heelstone and its Henge
Creates Father Sun's phallus-shadow. The
stone now leans inward at 20°, and the
henge is almost completely obliterated.

The Avenue
Now so faded it's hard
to see from ground level.
Added some centuries after
the main build, the inner bank
and outer ditch match that of the
original henge configuration. This
peculiarity is unseen anywhere else.

Both barrows represent Sister Moon
at her high and low standstill.

The single-ditched South Barrow was
built smaller than the North to avoid
impinging into the Southern Causeway.

The Station Stones long axes define the diameter
of Mother Earth and Father Sun's
orbit at either solstice.

* Though evidence-based, the symbolism expressed
on this page reflects my own interpretation.
It is not universally endorsed.

People who visit Stonehenge today often remark on the poor condition in which the monument finds itself. At right is a recent aerial of the entire henge. On the left side, the ditch and bank have melted into the ground, while in the lower right, the South Barrow can only been seen in the relief of late afternoon sun. The ditch and bank on the right side and Entrance are clearer only because of William Hawley's work in the northeast and south in the 1920s.

Gone are the days when visitors could simply pull over to the side of the road and picnic while wandering about the stones. With ticket sales in excess of a million units per year, the cumulative tromping of feet would devastate the site in short order. Small, strictly guided groups may obtain costly one-hour Special Access passes to the interior in morning or late afternoon, before or after regular daytime hours.

Open Access is granted only at solstice and equinox, and even this is being reviewed in light of some recent abuse. Except for a few cosmetic tweaks here and there, the site's overall condition has remained reasonably static since 1964, while a wide series of non-invasive upgrades were undertaken and completed in 2013 and -14.

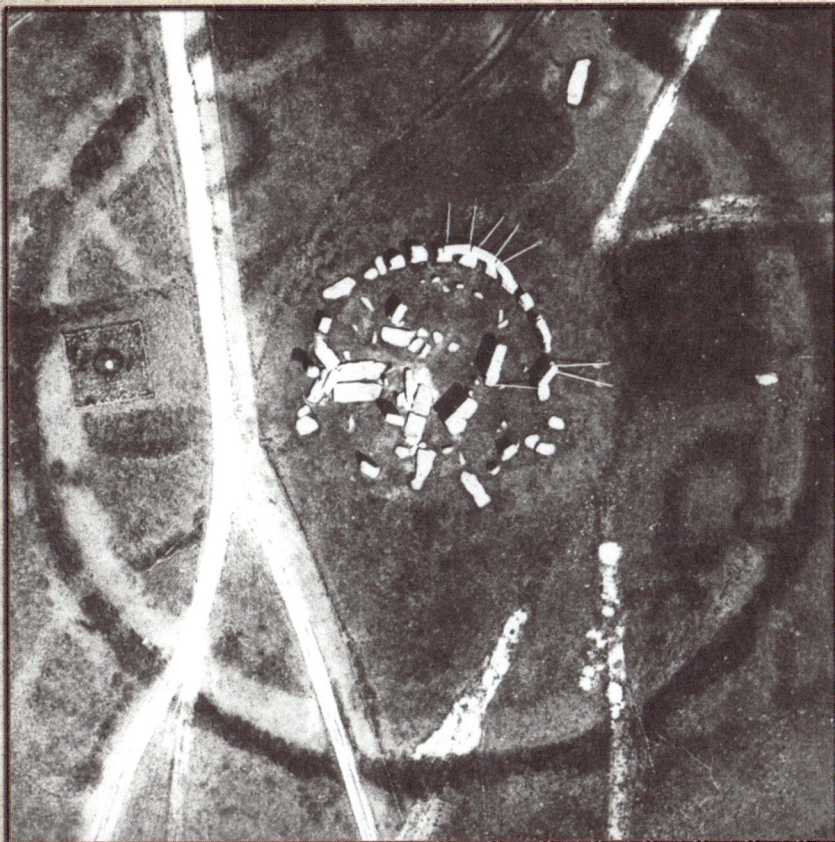

Below is an overhead taken in 1906 by Lt. Phillip Sharpe, from a series which represent the first aerial photographs of Stonehenge. To those who say the site has been abused, I urge a comparison.

No less than eight road-breaks impinge on the henge — and these are only the ones in use at the time; there are several older others. The white trails are caused by the turf being stripped away by travel, exposing the chalk underbed. The forked road at left is the original Byway-12, coming up from Normanton and passing through on its way to Larkhill. It's been moved west twice since that time. A wire fence along its east side ensured that visitors would pay the then very unpopular 2-shillings the owner insisted on charging. Today the admittance fee is US$25.00.

There's a fence around SS-93, and clearly seen is the fallen West Trilithon, with S-22 and broken L-122 laying across it. Eight larchwood poles support certain stones to prevent their inevitable collapse, and these were in place from 1904 until 1920.

While a variety of unintentional mistakes have been made over the years, these pictures show the site is currently in much better condition than it was a century ago.

One of the intentions of this book is to dispel some of the myths about Stonehenge and to articulate some new ideas, obviously with my own finding a vehicle. The reader with an editorial eye will notice that I haven't spent time with the tired premise of: 'I'm right / They're wrong', so common in this faceless digital age. This is not only a waste of time and space, but lumps the good in with the bad. There are a number of solid, evidence-based ideas out there that make sense. But there's a large balance of bad too, perpetrated by those who either haven't done much homework or neglect to examine glaring facts. A theory must be supported by *all* the information and we can't cherry-pick only that which fit a specific supposition. *(Believe me — I've heard some doozies!)* Rule Number One: Sift the evidence, *then* cook up an idea, because they don't just spring from the grass in whole crops. Ideas are sown, tilled, watered and weeded. A good example of fallow ground is it's possible the timber circles at Durrington were precursors to the grand works two miles away. So did they first build in wood at Stonehenge? Could be, but the evidence would have been destroyed by the installation of stones. So no one knows, except to say that the hand-crafted stone definitely mimics woodwork.

It appears that Stonehenge was a secret place — or what went on inside it was. The interior embankment was eight feet high: impossible to see over from downslope to the east and south. From higher ground to the north and west an eighteen foot tall Palisade was built of stout trees, running diagonally northeast from well below, then through the lower corner of the old visitor's car park, all the way to the Avenue's Elbow, as seen in Mr Dunn's map on page ten. This tightly woven screen was a mile long. What was going on in there?

Additionally, there is some slight evidence that much later there may have been a ring of shrubs set inside the earthwork, roughly positioned between the Y and Z Holes. *(I know — 'Stonehedge', right?)* So it seems that whatever was going on, a concerted effort was being made to keep prying eyes in the dark. This also speaks to a long-standing priestly class or what-not onto whom great influence was conferred, for one does not commit to the labor-costly equivalent of a Neolithic space program without some seriously strong imperative. We know that all governments have secrets. In many cases this is a good thing. That we *know* they have secrets has no bearing at all on whatever it is they're attempting to keep sub rosa. Stonehenge was surely no different.

There are any number of cremations scattered outside the Aubrey Holes; in the ditch and within the bank. Some are clustered together at key locations while others lie in isolation. Clearly, being laid to rest at this magickal place was a high honor. This is demonstrated when we examine the ashes, some of which are older than even the henge itself, meaning those remains had been curated for centuries before final disposition.

Long afterward, we see in one instance the remains of a certain unfortunate gentleman whose disarticulated skeleton was found in the north ditch in 1978. His interment was hardly ceremonial as he had no grave goods, and looks to have been simply tossed into a shallow cove and left to rot. Most telling however is that he didn't just keel over, but was killed with at least three arrows, possibly four. Two of these were loosed into him while he was already laying on the ground and are interpreted as coup d'grace kill-shots. His sole possession was a beautifully crafted stone wrist guard, suggesting he was himself an archer. This gruesome event appears to have occurred shortly after the stone phase at the monument had been completed. So who was this guy?

There are people I know who interpret this man as being a guardsman who bravely fought to protect the Citadel against the criminal element. Okay ... but it seems to me someone like that would be buried with honor. This guy? Not so much. I believe *he* was the spy, caught skulking around, killed for his effrontery, then chucked like a dog into the eternal empty. Bearing this curse, his abandoned soul would then wander forever in the bitter cold of Sister Moon's endless night. Thus the secrets of Stonehenge were protected from espionage.

That such measures were taken tell us that whatever was going on in there, the powers-that-be weren't fooling around with the silly strictures and folderol of legal red tape. If you got in there uninvited, you got dead — period. The locals would have known this and so avoided the place as though it were encircled by death itself.

Another burial in nearby West Amesbury tells a completely different tale. This grave contained an older man who was interred with reverent ceremony in a cist loaded with finely crafted items which include a cache of precious gold hair adornments. An archer in youth, he too died around the time the stones had been erected. His left kneecap is missing, caused by some tragic, painful mishap long before he passed, while an abcess in his jaw was so bad it may have been the final cause of death. In short, his last years were spent in a perpetual agony that we can scarcely imagine today. But what's more surprising is that he wasn't local-born. Strontium isotope tests reveal that he probably came from the Austrian Alps, over 750 miles away — a vast distance at that time.

The two archers died within 50-odd years of each other, but under utterly polarized circumstances. One was esteemed and had been welcomed into the community where he'd amassed valuables and social station. Later in life, suffering from painful affliction, was cared for. Of the local-born man we will never know much because he had nothing but the wrist guard. Murder? Intrigue? Espionage? Marvelous fodder for a prehistoric mystery novel, but baffling to those seeking answers. The only thing the two men have in common of course, is Stonehenge itself. So what could be the lure which drew the older man, and presumably others, from such distance?

In 2008, rare permission was granted for a small excavation within the Sarsen Circle itself for the first time in half a century. Respected professors Tim Darvill and Geoff Wainwright were pursuing a theory which held that the bluestones had been thought to possess mystical healing properties and Stonehenge had morphed into a kind of Bronze Age Lourdes. It was surmised that people came from near and far to benefit from this miracle.

In addition to many interesting finds, the upper layers of the dig exposed a large number of bluestone chips that seem to have been struck off the stones where they stood. It's thought people came and took away amulets to aid their health. Similar chips are also found within this so-called Stonehenge Layer in the ditch, bank, Y & Z holes and other places in- and outside the henge. This is offered as an explanation for why so many bluestones are now only stumps below the surface. So our ill-fated, skulking young man obviously snuck in to steal some of these magick healing stones.

To my ears, this otherwise provocative theory sounds a little thin, in that we can safely assume that the Citadel was under strict control. They wouldn't be letting old Aunt Gertrude in to bash a bluestone because she suffered from a touch of arthritis. Plus, it seems odd that there's still so many slivers there if they were intended as talismans of health or good fortune. I believe the luckless Stonehenge Archer came to steal *ideas* — not artifacts.

As far as the old man is concerned, well — this period had become a different and important time. In the middle of the second millennia BCE metal was coming into vogue. The Chalcolithic, or Copper Age had been sweeping across Europe for quite a while and by the time the sarsens were being erected had found its way to England. We see its development in tools and weapons, and though useless for stonework, was no doubt present. Soon it was found that blending copper with tin created bronze and they were off and running. A youthful Amesbury Archer had come with European traders and remained. Verdict: *No connection between our adventurers.*

It's my belief that the introduction of metal affected all cultures in a fundamental way. Here's a material that has actual value as well as use, so no longer did the leader have to be the biggest, strongest, or smartest — he merely needed more assets than his peers. As stone implements graduated to the copper and bronze variety, this influence could alter a perception of the very gods themselves. If those in power reinterpret the deity to their advantage, they can easily subjugate a populace with the penalties or rewards of cold hard cash. The most obvious dividend of this is sponsored violence. Metal makes money, money makes greed, greed makes war. Now throw someone's Almighty into the mix and watch the fun. The negative effects of this insidious formula continue with few changes into the present day.

———————————————●———————————————

ABOVE: *The dignified interment of the so-called Amesbury Archer. An older gent of high status, he had a missing left kneecap and suffered a jaw abcess so infected it probably contributed to his death. His is among the most richly appointed graves ever found from this period.*

RIGHT: *Wiltshire Museum display of the skeleton found in the north ditch. Killed by at least 3 arrows, his disheveled position tells us that he was just thrown in and left to rot. Burrowing creatures have further disturbed his remains.*

On some level the people who lived in ancient times were no doubt aware that information couldn't be transmitted intact to later generations; that is: write an instructional leaflet. So what they built to illustrate concepts had to be understood by whom it was intended. We merely have to decipher what they were thinking and we'll have all the answers. Sounds easy. Now do it in phonetic Chinese with half the alphabet missing.

We do not have — and probably never will — the equivalent of a 5,000-year-old Rosetta Stone to assist in the nuance of a culture for which we have limited reference. All we can do is keep searching for clues that help us understand what was, to them, an obvious thing. Some answers we shall never have, but some indirect instances are common with what we see in building projects today. One of the things about Stonehenge which emphasizes the humanistic scope is that a few mistakes were made in its execution. None are game changers, but required a workaround to correct the error and salvage any invested labor from being reproduced.

These errors are helpful in determining various methods of construction, frequently to the exclusion of other theories. In 2012 a meticulous series of laser scans were performed on every stone at the complex, down to half a millimeter. These data have challenged some ideas we had in several areas, but also aided in putting a face on individual components: i.e. a feature in thus or such section can only have been performed by one person at a time as they scrubbed the stone with a round sarsen ball. Left-handed / right-handed / master / apprentice, or the layering of rough work under finish have all been detected with this fascinating forensic technique.

A rare earthquake occurred about a thousand years ago and this probably brought down Stone-55 of the Great Trilithon. In the collapse, Lintel-156 was yanked from the tenon of S-56 and this surely began the process of its famous lean over the years. Sadly, S-55 broke in two when it fell and the lintel was flung down across the Altar Stone. It now lies on what was its northeast face with the two deep mortise holes plainly exposed for all to see.

But what's that on the other side? Two partial gouges appear on what was the top of the lintel, positioned near either end. What are *these* for? Vectored landing beacons for the Alien Mothership? Neolithic smoke pots? A pair of bird baths? Nope. They're errors committed on one of the most important stones in the Horseshoe.

So a couple of young apprentices are working this big slab for a week until some middle-management suit wanders by and tells them they're banging on the wrong side. They have to flip the stone over and start all over again — but you know those poor kids are gouging holes in the chalk with an antler pick the next day …

Over on the west side, circle Stone-21 was shaped and erected like all the others, but when they hoisted the lintel between it and S-22 they bashed the upper inside face and detached a large chunk of the saddle, taking half the tenon with it. A new lintel had to be crafted with more widely spaced mortises cut into it. *Whoopsey!*

As mentioned, the lintels are curved and have alternate lock-joints in the ends; one intruding, one extruding. These stones were likely mass-produced with only the mortises custom fit. I suspect separate crews worked on either end. As these stones travel along the now-incomplete eastern circle we see that one lintel must have had intrusions on *both* ends. Because of the precisely determined length, in addition to the stone's graceful curve, it cannot have been reversed or modified, so had to be replaced by a new, corrected version. The shop steward for Stone Banger's Local 101 was called to the site-office. *Here's your antler pick. Have a nice day …*

In 1953, at the outset of some intensive excavations, Richard Atkinson was walking the interior south side of the Horseshoe. It must have been mid-afternoon as the slanting sun revealed what remains among the intriguing mysteries at Stonehenge. On the face of the South Trilithon's Stone-53, at eye level, is an incised line of graffito, and while this feature is interesting, it pales compared to what appears below it. Obscured in direct light, but seen in relief, are two carvings which must be near-original. One is a dagger, the other an axe.

Copious photos were taken, heads were shaken and hands were wrung. What were these marks *for?* In time, about 60 were found on various stones throughout the complex, with the largest concentration of them on the exterior of Stone-4. All but three are axes and all were carved sequentially over a period of many years. None of them overlap. Some are plain as day once you know they're there while others can only be seen in a certain light. The laser scans increased the number to a remarkable 115, with some so worn they're nearly invisible.

One hint may lie on Stone-4, where over half — 59 in total — are found. The cardinal east line skims the north side of this stone and as we've determined, east is the direction from whence life originates. Do they record the passage of royalty? If so, the lineage is long. Are they the number of eclipses witnessed from the Citadel, or perhaps a thousand-year catalog of lunar standstills? I have the distinct impression that we will never know.

Lintel-156 lies on its northeast face straddling the Altar Stone. The deep mortices are clearly visible on what was once its underside. The rear hole is for the tenon on Stone-56, standing behind.

The dagger & axe carvings on Stone-53. Officially discovered in 1953, they are now seen in photographs dating back to the 1860s.

RIGHT: *The opposite side, or top of Lintel-156 showing the two partial mortice-gouges. Notice the rough finish on what was once the top, never intended to be seen from the ground. This, in addition to the graceful arc, indicate that the mortices could only have been oriented correctly with the other face down.*
Somebody goofed!
It lies across BS-67 on the right, while the sharp-eyed will detect the Altar Stone tucked in under its center.

Below is a drawing of the 59 axe carvings on Stone-4. This concentration of marks may be significant as they appear almost directly on the cardinal east line.

Stone-21 of the west Sarsen Circle. Notice the sharp angle at the interior top. This is breakage caused by the lintel bashing the stone while being lifted into position.

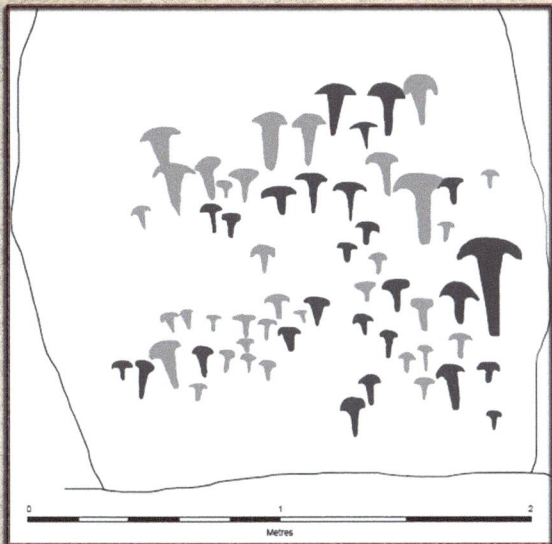

The underside of L-101. This lintel has been shaved at its seats to maintain a level top.

A controversial aspect at Stonehenge concerns the restorations of the 20th century. While these episodes were neither conducted in secret nor design-altering, it's perhaps regrettable that later visitors were given the impression that the stones were in original condition. To be fair, though the State avoided mention of these events for years, the projects were never actually denied. While the motivation for this silence might be subject to a variety of interpretations, I think it's time to move on from errors of the past, either real or imagined.

The repair process began back in 1880 with a survey by William Flinders Petrie, whose numbering system remains in use. In 1893 the Inspector of Ancient Monuments reported that several stones were in danger of collapse, and this was underscored seven years later when Stone-22 came crashing down in a terrific winter gale on New Year's Eve 1900. The upright itself was none the worse for wear, but Lintel-122 broke in two.

In early 1901 Lord Edmund Antrobus, the property's owner, directed a committee of Wiltshire antiquarians to devise a plan of preservation. William Gowland was retained: a metallurgist recently returned from Japan after years spent studying Shinto sites. One impetus for the limited work might be calculated by expense, but the result was that only Stone-56 was to be reset. To recover costs, a fee of two shillings was levied upon visitors. Gowland set about this task in September 1901, carefully lifting, excavating and re-setting the mighty stone to within inches of its presumed original position. Now locked in a concrete caisson, it will never move again. Though not an archaeologist in the strictest sense, Professor Gowland's research and interpretation added a thick chapter to the thin pamphlet of extant Stonehenge knowledge, while his methods are still admired.

In 1915, for digressive reasons, Stonehenge and its surrounding acres were sold at public auction to local man Cecil Chubb, who bought it to prevent rich Americans from getting their grubby paws on the iconic stones. He gave it to the Crown three years later. Delivered to the Office of Works, under whose aegis all work was carried out, the complex was surveyed to the inch in 1919. These plans are so accurate that, with updates, Ros Cleal and her team used them in 1995s essential: *Stonehenge in its Landscape*, the touchstone for all serious researchers of the monument. They're at the root of my own humble drawings in this book, made with grubby paws.

Between 1920 and 1927, the site was relentlessly overrun by Lt Col William Hawley, who had worked with Gowland years earlier. Not really a Colonel or even an archaeologist, Hawley has taken a lot of heat for the bull-in-a-china-shop approach to excavation, and some of it is merited. Though the invasive techniques produced results, the devastation he wrought can never be repaired and crucial information has been lost forever. The heavy-handed actions are no justification for the recovery of an antler pick or a few Roman coins. I'm exaggerating, but only slightly, as the entire east and south interior was virtually bulldozed. He found the postholes and the forgotten Aubreys, while several key elements were identified at the entrance, along with a number of cremations in the ditch and bank. Stones -6 and -7 were readjusted and he pushed the four Aperture Stones back into place, enabling the removal of the eight support poles which for years had made the site look so shabby. But Hawley's notes were deeply remiss and he never published his findings in a cohesive fashion.

In 1950, a trio of noted archaeologists led by Richard JC Atkinson began an extended course of examination which pushed our knowledge of Stonehenge far beyond what had been known. An accurate approximation of its age, the major phases of construction, and the lengths of time between are only a few advancements among many. Atkinson has also left us a legacy of over 2,000 photographs from their on and off 13 years of research.

1958 saw the task of lifting the West Trilithon. Two cranes were brought in — one a standard workhorse, the other a huge Brabazon aircraft crane borrowed from the RAF. Rated to 60 tons, it was the only machine powerful enough to get the job done. Clearing S-22 and broken L-122, the Trilithon stones were lifted aside, exposing a broad swath of the surface. The entire area was then screened down to the chalk — literally by the teaspoon. The dig reports read like a forensic spreadsheet, such is the watershed of information.

Stone-22 was re-erected, and L-122, repaired with steel rods, was slung into place atop S-21 and -22. Then a large concrete vault was formed in the ground and each Trilithon upright was lowered into prepared slots, positioned precisely as they had been originally — thanks in large part to William Stukeley's 230-year old illustrations. Onlooking crowds, newsreel- and still-cameras watched a battered Lintel-158 raised, lowered and shimmed to the stack. With this facelift Stonehenge recovered a large fragment of its compromised dignity.

1964's treatment saw new-fallen S-23 re-set, along with several bluestones. Stones -4, -5, -28 and -29 were also righted. The massive South Trilithon was encased in a steel frame and after excavation was winched up straight. Unsightly mud-retarding gravel was introduced to the interior in the mid-1960s, but then removed in the late 1970s. Apart from a few cosmetic upgrades over the years the site has remained relatively unscathed.

LEFT: *c.1881. This John Jenkins Cole photo shows Stone-56 leaning hard over onto BS-68. This is one of a series of pictures used to illustrate the site's poor condition at the time. Chalk graffiti can be seen on many stones.*

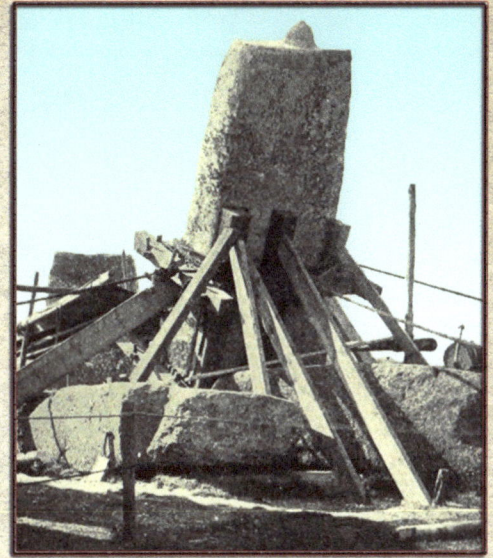

RIGHT: *Sept. 1901. William Gowland's timber yoke and struts encase Stone-56 as it's pushed upright. His excavations recovered a trove of important information.*

RIGHT: *c.1920. William Hawley's crew lifts the lintel from leaning Stones -6 and -7, preparing to straighten them. After fifteen years the shabby looking poles were removed from seven various uprights. In all, Hawley righted six stones, the sockets of which were excavated, then used as concrete forms.*

BELOW: *May 1958. Stonehenge enters the Space Age! In fear that a bedding plane shear might destroy Stone-58 in the lift, a portable X-Ray machine was recruited to examine it, seen as the suspended keg-shaped device. Three 3-inch holes were cored through the upper, middle, and lower face of the shear, with threaded steel rods slotted into them. The 6 plugging inserts are visible today — some of which are mismatched to their holes.*

BELOW RIGHT: *Sept. 1958. The borrowed RAF Brabazon aircraft crane was taxed to its limit lifting the two 40-ton uprights. Laying across the fallen standers for 161 years, Lintel-158 is being hoisted back to its perch high atop the restored West Trilithon.*

Many of the fanciful names given to various stones or locations in the vicinity grew from superstition, adopted long before the true nature of the feature was fully understood. Each of these antique titles usually has a colorful tale associated with it.

ABOVE: *The fallen Slaughter Stone. The pit in which it lies may either reflect attempts to bury it in antiquity, or perhaps a failure to replace the fill when it was excavated in 1812. Pooling rainwater oxidizes its high iron content, giving rise to the persistent, age old myth of bloody human sacrifice!*

TOP RIGHT: *Bluestone-150 rests beneath BS-32. The 2 mortices tell of an earlier stint as a lintel in the Q & R double circle setting, but it was later reused in the outer ring.*

LEFT: *Station Stone-93 sits alone out on the west henge perimeter.*

LEFT: *Station Stone-91 slumps against the east embankment.*

RIGHT: *Almost certainly the oldest sarsen at the site, the undressed 28-ton Heelstone now leans inward at 20-degrees. Sixteen feet tall, its opposite, or west side, marks the axis of summer solstice.*

Below is the original, incorrect north/south cardinal passing through the center of the henge, the South Trilithon's S-54, S-11, Aubrey Hole-20, and then out to bisect the Southern Causeway. The true line passes from a similar center, but crosses just to the left of the west ditch terminal.

BELOW: *Stone-28 glowers imperiously.*

ABOVE: *The words SEDGFIELD ANSTEF are seen on Stone-23. Whether a name, an acronym or both, it's an odd moniker. They're cut over the earlier date of 1817.*

TOP LEFT: *The last carving at the site before new laws prevented desecration. H BRIDGER 1866 Chi Sux is found on the exterior of Stone-5. Mr Bridger was from Chichester in Sussex and can still be found in period census rolls.*

MIDDLE LEFT: *Surrounded by lesser examples, at eye-level on Trilithon Stone-53, is the deeply incised carving which for years was thought to be in Latin. Chiseled by a right-handed person we see:*
·IOH: LVD: DEFFERRE·
Tenuous evidence suggests a Frenchman named John Louis Deferre may have visited Amesbury in 1755. He must have been on an extended tour as this inscription would have taken quite a while to complete.

ABOVE MIDDLE: *Broken Stone 55-a provided a convenient seat while carving many remembrances into the ages.*

LEFT: *Noted architect Sir Christopher Wren retreated to his native Wiltshire after the Great London Fire of 1666. Sammy Glastonbury and her father view clear evidence of Wren's visit on Stone-52.*

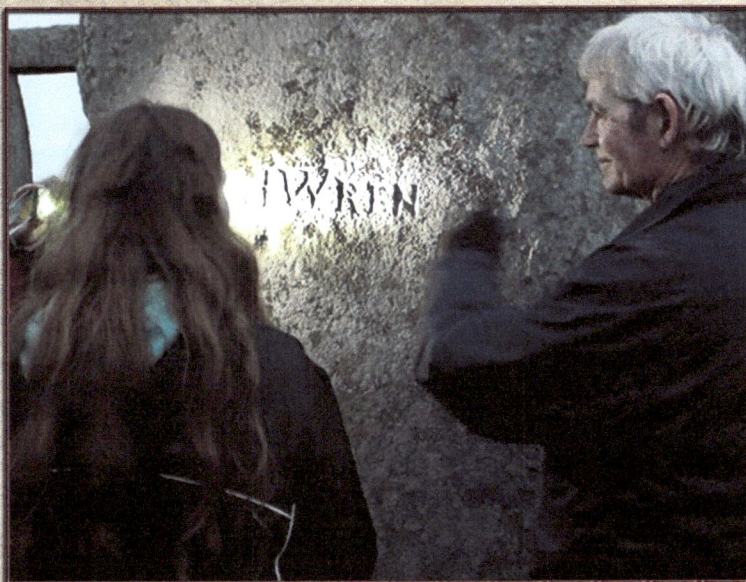

What Became of the Missing Stones?

Thirty-five of the upright sarsen stones remain of forty originals. Twenty-six are standing, nine are fallen or broken, and five are missing altogether. The previously undetected sockets for Stones -17 & -18 were discovered in 2013, so these are accounted for, if only as placeholders.

Only 44 bluestones remain out of 90 or so originals. Thirteen stand while the rest are prone or buried.

The largest percentage of missing stones are the lintels, with only 13 of 40 originals on-site. Nine sit in place, 4 are fallen; the others long gone. Out of an estimated 165 original stones, only 92 remain.

Twenty-one of the stones have been manipulated in one way or another during the restoration projects of the 20th century, though according to an admittedly sketchy historical record, nothing at Stonehenge has been robbed within at least the last 500 years or more. While 40% of the stones are missing, the greatest bulk of these have been the smallest of them. Only five of the outer sarsen orthostats are gone altogether and none of the Trilithons are absent.

There are several possible reasons for this. Though still quite massive, the outer stones would have been far easier to manage than the Trilithons. Not only would those ten megaliths be enormously cumbersome to man-handle, but retrieving the broken pieces from inside would only compound the difficulties. So even with the use of firepits and water, such as was used at Avebury in the 14th century, this common, efficient method would have been particularly arduous if performed within the relatively cramped confines of the stone circle.

But there is no evidence of firepits at Stonehenge. The Slaughter Stone *does* display signs of a process called plug-and-feathering, which is a series of small holes drilled in a line, creating a fracture along which a rock can be broken. It's the only one with such holes and the task was never completed. That process would have ruined expensive drills, meaning that perhaps the tough stone itself defeated the robbers. Alternatively, this effort may have seen more success on other stones, with gangs taking those instead, leaving the Slaughter Stone behind.

All that being said, I believe only previously fallen stones were robbed, this being the path of least resistance. The same earthquake that brought down Stone-55 no doubt caused the collapse of others. Several of these are only remnants; evidence of easy picking. S-8, -9, -15 and -19 are the examples. Stones -12 and -25 likely fell after the robbing period, while the slow decline of -14 is chronicled in several pieces of artwork through the 18th and 19th centuries, explaining why those three are more or less intact. None of the standers in the northeast are missing or broken, and though those four stones did eventually require adjustment, we know that the ones in the southwest were of less quality and, having shallow sockets, more readily succumbed to the ravages of time and tempest. Lintels scattered by fallen uprights could be collected without too much fuss, while the balance of others could have been brought down by a team of stout draft horses and good rope.

The fact remains that there's no trace of sarsen or bluestone at any farm, inn, village, estate or home within a considerable radius from the site. No foundations, bridges or garden arrangements in the area are crafted from the missing material, which seems strange as it could have become a handy rock quarry for the entire region.

So we go further back in time. While there's no evidence, the Romans may have done it during their long occupation of Britain. There are hints they took more than a passing interest in the site and might have rearranged a few of the bluestones. Also, the condition of S-11 is suspicious, as it tips into its erection ramp, suggesting an effort to pull it down. The upper third snapped off, they took it away, and left the remainder leaning out.

Alas, the Romans left us no record. But extraordinary by omission, there is little mention of *any* major monument throughout the vast Roman Empire, so this one is hardly an exception. Being famously accomplished, highly organized engineers, they could have easily broken the stones up and carted the rubble off to distant projects which are now vanished into misty, historically mundane venues, leaving none the wiser today.

As it's become increasingly clear that Stonehenge was completed, the real puzzle is that there's no clue where the 70-odd lost stones might have gotten off to, and this has driven sane men mad.   *Where's my pills …*

As you might imagine, there have been a great number of investigations at Stonehenge over the centuries. The people who conducted these range in expertise from bored picnickers chipping at the stones, to some of the most renown archaeologists in history. The earliest of these will remain forever anonymous, detected only by finding their crude disturbances under the soil. A brief description of a few of the more well regarded follows.

Inigo Jones 1573 - 1652. At the behest of King Charles I, noted architect and theatrical designer Inigo Jones investigated the site, then wrote a book entitled: *Stone-Heng Restored* in which he asserts the structure was either a Roman temple, or at least of Tuscan design. His illustrations are finely executed, but convinced that Stonehenge was of classical origin, he added features that were never there, such as a sixth Trilithon.

John Aubrey 1626 - 1697. An antiquary, natural philosopher, writer and historian, Aubrey also engaged in the rudiments of archaeology. He is credited with major discoveries at Avebury, while the Aubrey Holes at Stonehenge are named after him — perhaps erroneously. On friendly terms with many of the day's best thinkers, most of his work was never published during his lifetime. Long considered an entertaining but quirky social gossip, only quite recently has his work been viewed as more important than originally thought.

Dr William Stukeley 1687 - 1765. Though incorrectly attributing Stonehenge to the druids, Stukeley nevertheless remains a driving force in the early study of the monument. A pioneer in archaeological investigation, he worked for nearly twenty years in and around the monument making observations, discoveries and cataloguing finds. Still well considered, his detailed illustrations assisted in re-erecting the West Trilithon in 1958.

Richard Colt Hoare 1758 - 1838. From a well-connected family of great personal resource, Colt Hoare is among the more interesting and diverse personalities of all investigators. He funded and personally assisted William Cunnington in two digs at Stonehenge. The first was in 1798, where the newly collapsed West Trilithon was inspected, and then in 1812 when the Slaughter Stone was excavated. *They're the ones who stashed the bottle of port*. Additionally, he and Cunnington catalogued 379 barrows out on the Salisbury Plain, while identifying many other prehistoric features in the area. He published *The Ancient History of Wiltshire* in two volumes.

William Gowland 1842 - 1922. Despite having no formal archaeological training, Gowland produced some of the most detailed records ever made at Stonehenge. Retained by the property owner through the Wiltshire Antiquarian Society, in his mandate he righted perilously leaning Stone-56, established that antler picks had been used to dig the stone holes, and that the stones had been shaped on site.

William Hawley 1851 - 1941. His work identified the Aubrey Holes, the Y & Z Holes and a variety of post- and stone holes within the monument. He found inhumations and cremated remains, which was the first indication of a funerary role for Stonehenge. Though important, his heavy handed methods are widely criticized today.

Richard JC Atkinson 1920 - 1994. Professor Atkinson directed all the excavations at Stonehenge between 1950 and 1964. With Stuart Piggott and John Stone (until Stone's death in 1957) he conducted the most comprehensive investigation within the earthwork. Instrumental in re-erecting the West Trilithon, he also oversaw the righting of numerous other stones. His records are also fragmentary, but Atkinson's legacy remains long.

Lance and Faith Vatcher. This husband and wife team worked at Durrington and Woodhenge in the 1960s and 70s, then went on to discover the Car Park Totems, the north ditch skeleton and the mysterious chalk plaques.

Mike Pitts 1950—. Directing emergency excavations at Stonehenge in 1979 / 80, his roadside trench revealed the socket for Stone-97. Now a senior editor for British Archaeology magazine, he acts as something of a clearing house for Stonehenge information along with many other sites and subjects.

Julian Richards 1951—. In 1980 Richards joined Wessex Archaeology and ran the Stonehenge Environs Project, a detailed study of Stonehenge and its surrounding landscape. Excavations at nearby Coneybury Henge revealed that the area had been occupied for several thousand years before Stonehenge was built. Sliding into a career as a popular television personality, Richards' important early work is sometimes overlooked.

Mike Parker-Pearson 1957—. From 2003 through 2009, he helmed the Stonehenge Riverside Project, where his large team discovered a new henge site at the River Avon. In addition to excavations at Durrington Walls and 35 other locations in the area, he oversaw the re-opening of Aubrey -7. His views are widely seen as the cornerstone of current thinking on Stonehenge, though death as its theme and its function as a unifying factor in the regional culture are being revised. For the last few years he has been searching Craig Rhos-y-fellin and other outcrops in Wales for the source of the Stonehenge bluestones, and there's been some success.

A number of things I have inserted into this book are new, or, to my knowledge, no one else has thought of before — which would be an extraordinary thing indeed. The layout squares, the real vs false cardinals, Aubrey oppositions, the quarter-season observances, and the Newgrange/summer sunset alignment all seem to be original. My ideas about a male Sun, female Earth and Sun's Sister Moon are not a long stretch from other standpoints, but I believe the deities were personified rather than idealized, as is contended elsewhere.

The idea that Stonehenge represented a geocentric cosmos has been catching on recently, and while I have been a long-time proponent of the theory, Jon Morris brings it to a new level with his fascinating premise. We have collaborated over the years and, though he continues his thesis beyond mine, we stroll down the same path together for quite a while before parting with a handshake. Which is to say, if you follow what I have done here, you'll slip very comfortably into what he does there. I highly recommend his *Stonehenge: Solving the Neolithic Universe*, for it truly does 'Blow the Lid Off' most ideas about the monument.

There's my shameless plug for an exceptionally good book.

The diagram below shows one of the most enigmatic associations I've ever seen in all my years of studying this monument. Long after the interior stone arrangement had been completed and the Avenue built, other features appeared in the vicinity during the Bronze and Iron Ages. By far the greatest number of these are barrows, and most remain respectfully distant from Stonehenge. (Even though, curiously, virtually all of them have easy sightlines to it.) But there are three or four within a stone's throw, and the closest two of these are highlighted.

The older of them is the Amesbury-10 disc barrow, which lies precisely 3 on-center henge diameters southwest, and is centered exactly on the Stone-97 axis. It appears to be a double-ditched feature, is slightly oval, and shows evidence of pits or burials in the center. Its short-axis diameter is identical to the Sarsen Circle.

I believe the A-10 represents the setting winter sun and is inaccurately dated. If more recent, how could the designers have mucked up its axis when the Avenue would be a natural guide? How would they have known the position of long-absent Stone-97? Therefore I submit that it's an original feature built *with* Stonehenge, but its style and near proximity are what make the presumption of a later date. Ground radar examined it in 1994 but no deposits have ever been recovered. (If I'm right, they'll find cremation charcoal in those central pits.)

The A-11 Bell Barrow was built in the late Bronze- or early Iron Age. Though most likely intended as a tomb, only one human finger bone has been recovered. It lies one henge diameter away from Stonehenge, rim-to-rim, and one on-center diameter from the major south moonrise. It seems to scale from the solstice axis, as its center occurs at 51° from that line. *Does that number sound familiar?* From the southwest side, the summer solstice sunset intersects the Heelstone. The diameter of the interior bell also is identical to the Sarsen Circle. I believe this feature represents the moon and is correctly dated, as it's positioned by earth, moon and sun axes.

Although this curious little chestnut appears toward the end of the book, it's the main observation which prompted my writing it in the first place.

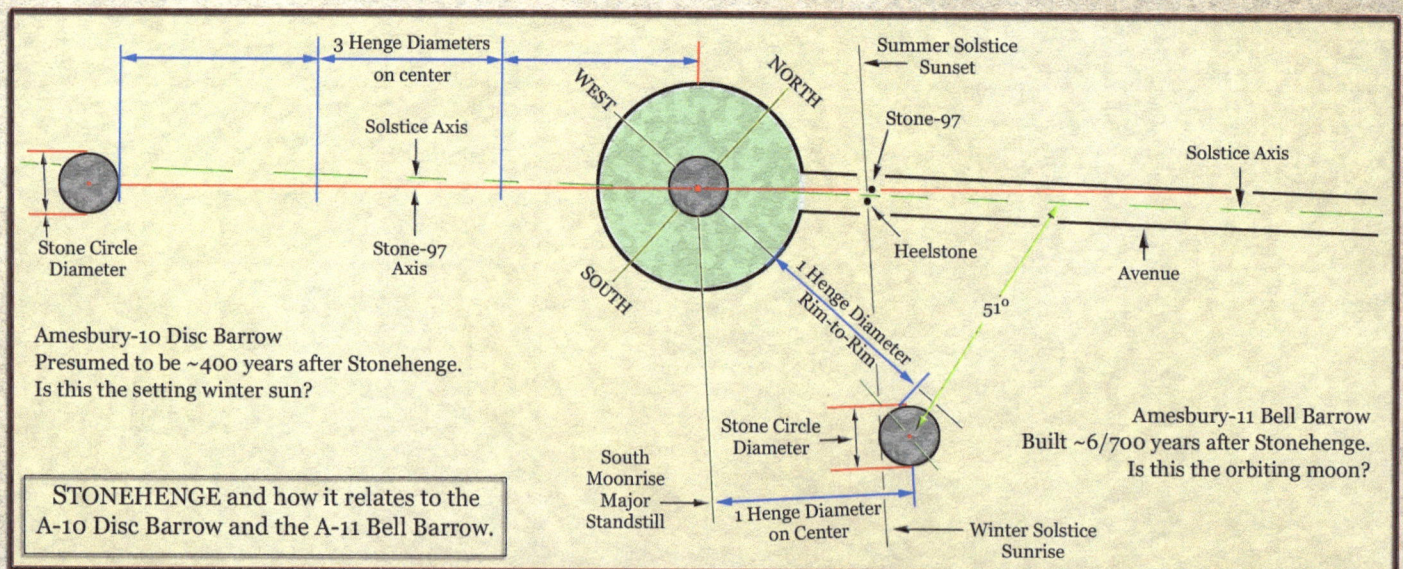

STONEHENGE and how it relates to the A-10 Disc Barrow and the A-11 Bell Barrow.

The A-10 disc barrow, the A-11 bell barrow and Stonehenge in context.

For all our advances and in spite of huge gains in information provided by the work done since 2003, the previous page details the stark reality of what Stonehenge still clutches tightly, her ancient secrets jealously hidden from prying eyes, never to be revealed.

The key to understanding the Neolithic will always rest with the people who lived in that time. But they are diaphanous wisps — formless shadows hovering at the fringe of our perception, akin to bleached, dog-eared snapshots briefly glimpsed in some dusty attic scrapbook. Indirectly backlit by a dearth of clues left behind, we find the broken tool, a random shard of grooved ceramic, or the bone pin from a disintegrated leather bag. But their homes are little more than etchings in the chalk, while tattered hints at clothing or shoes say nothing of those who wore them. The words spoken to instruct, cajole or convey a tender sentiment linger in the ether as soundless, forgotten enigmas. They made music, but we shall never hear it. Their art has vanished forever.

We have a few graves, some of their remains and the odd heirloom, but these tell us little of how they lived, what they thought, or where their inspiration might have taken them. A single chalk-carved pig — a child's toy — has become the age's poignant icon, yet serves to cast vacant innuendo at the things we share in common. They laughed, loved, cried and dreamed. Huddled clutches of teenaged girls swooned at boastful young men's bravado while ever-watchful matrons gossiped on. Wise grandparents eternally dispensed unheeded advice ...

They certainly had a social caste system, but while we can read the humorous, often blasphemous, graffiti left by the masons of Babylon, Sumeria and Egypt, how the toiling folk of the Stonehenge era felt about their princes, overlords, neighbors or kin are a blank entry in history's ledger, and always will be.

What became of them? Were they swept away in catastrophe; destroyed by invasion? Were they ravaged by plague or did their static culture simply turn in on itself? No one had been able to address these questions.

We finally have that answer and it's deceptively simple. Twice before you've read mention of a certain means of identification — through the detection of strontium isotopes found in all carbon-based life. When skeletons are recovered we can often determine not just the DNA signature of the individual, but where they were born. This method uses a process whereby the oxygen in tooth enamel is examined, which sources the water that was drunk in early life. The minerals within can then be differentiated literally on a map. This has been done with startling results, with not the least example being the 2002 discovery of the Amesbury Archer, known by this ingenious application to have come all the way from Austria. Julian Richards, in his popular television program *Meet the Ancestors*, used DNA sampling and the strontium process to make yet another startling discovery.

The people who lived in the time of Stonehenge didn't commit mass suicide, weren't conquered, devastated by plague, or perish in the nightmare of a sunless nuclear winter.

They're all still there. The farmers, shopkeepers, carpenters and candlestick makers around the wide region are direct, lineal descendants of the builders of Stonehenge, inextricably woven into the fabric of the land itself.

So the next time you're in Amesbury looking for a cold-chisel to carve your name on those hoary old grey-weathers, be sure and ask the clerk what the devil all those pesky daggers and axes are supposed to mean!

From pithy and banal to sublime or sophomoric, Stonehenge across the ages has been described, depicted and grandly theorized about by many. But whether it was known as Chorea Gigantum, Sten Heng, Chior Ghaur, or the Giant's Dance, it has piqued the imagination of all who have beheld it.

Speculation about its meaning and purpose continue to the present day and it remains high on the list of the top ten most photographed subjects of the world.

Here are some selected renditions over a span of five hundred years. The conspiricists who claim it was built in the 1950s have some explaining to do!

Dr William Stukeley as a druid in 1740.

Scholarly gossip John Aubrey in 1666.

1535 by DeHeere. RIGHT: *1480. Merlin builds the Giant's Round, as described by Geoffrey of Monmouth in 1136.*

ABOVE: *Surprisingly lucid for 1635.*

ABOVE: *The Domesday manuscript c.1250. c.1575 woodcut with castle in background.*

Stukeley 1727

STONHING

STONEHENGE
Relative Stone Heights

Measurements reflect altitudes above ground.
Depths below ground are widely variable.

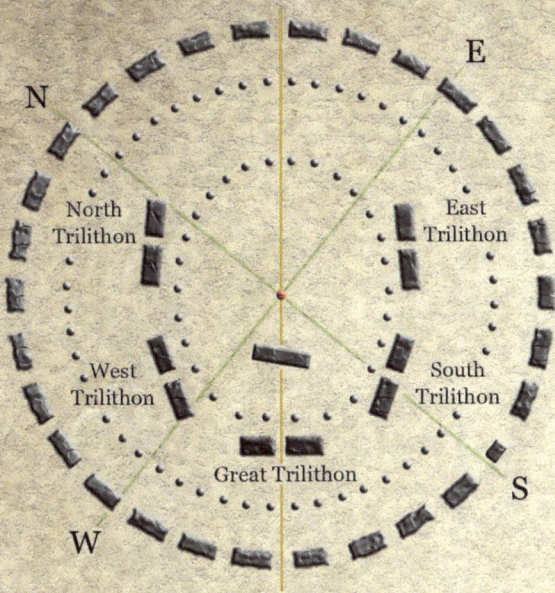

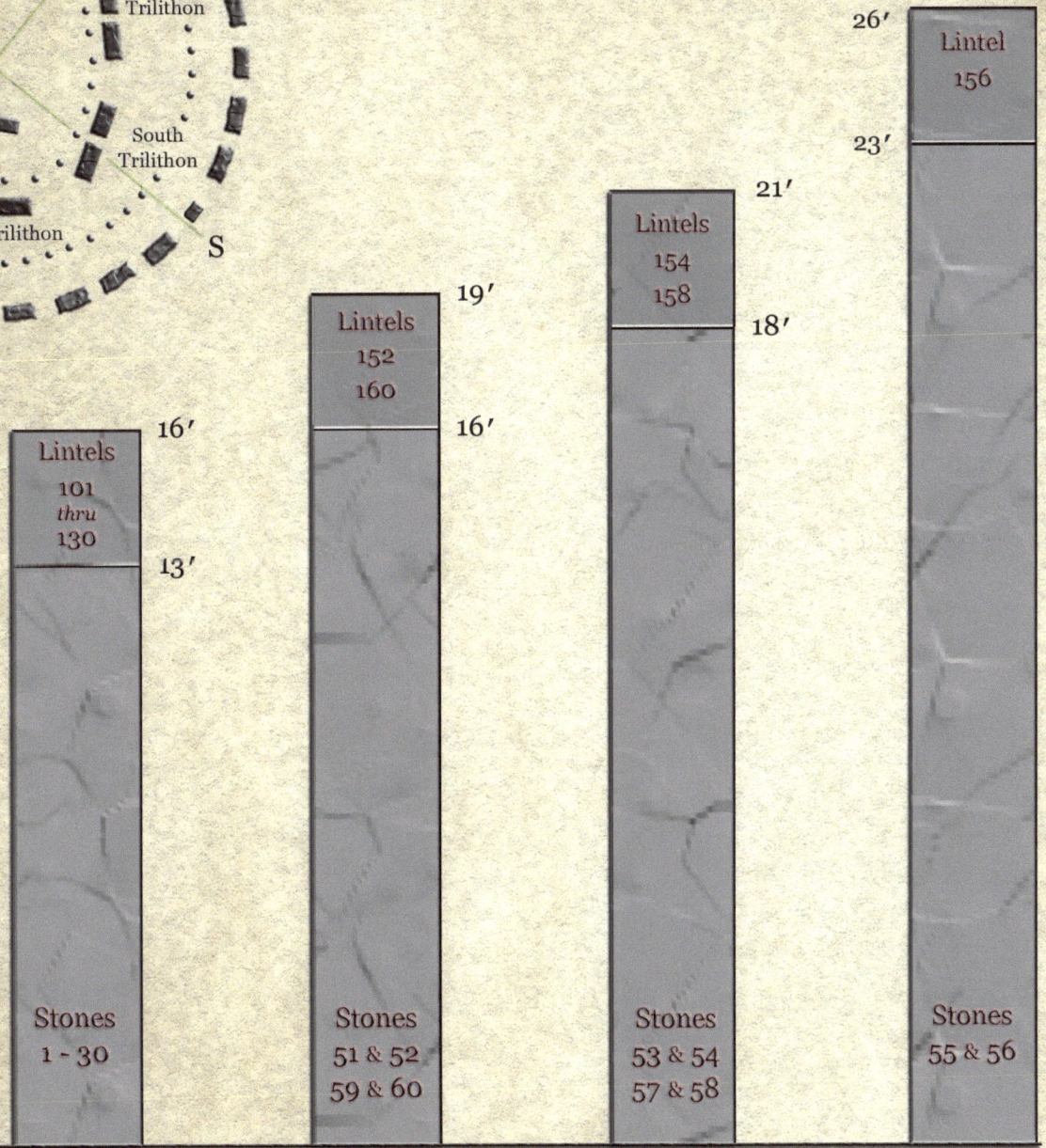

N

E

North
Trilithon

East
Trilithon

West
Trilithon

South
Trilithon

Great Trilithon

S

W

26'

Lintel
156

23'

21'

Lintels
154
158

18'

19'

Lintels
152
160

16'

16'

Lintels
101
thru
130

13'

Human
to Scale

Stones
1 - 30

Stones
51 & 52
59 & 60

Stones
53 & 54
57 & 58

Stones
55 & 56

Circle Bluestone	Trilithon Bluestone	Standard Circle Stone	East & North Trilithons	South & West Trilithons	Great Trilithon

Lintel lengths are variable depending on location. The Stone Circle lintels average
10-feet 6-inches, except at the northeast entrance and its southwest counterpart.
Those uprights are spaced farther apart to accommodate the sun's passage
through, so their lintels are correspondingly longer.

The Trilithon lintels are balanced in size according to the height of their uprights.
The North and East Trilithon capstones are fourteen feet long. The South and West's
are almost fifteen feet, while the Great Trilithon's lintel is slightly more than sixteen.

Cover: Adam Stanford (*Incredibly difficult decision with so many of Adam's selections to choose from. Then he tossed this one out, saying: "How about this old thing?" I never looked back ...*)

Sarsen Circle plan: After Anthony Johnson, 2008.

Title: Frank Stevens. (*This manipulated 1922 woodcut is clever, but historically impossible.*)

Preface Page: Original: Pete Glastonbury.

Page 1: Pete Glastonbury.

Page 3: Map: Wikipedia.

Page 4: Windmill Hill, Devil's Den, Cursus Barrows: Pete Glastonbury. Woodhenge: Adam Stanford. Ring of Brodgar, Drombeg, Castelrigg: Unknown. Bush Barrow, Stonehenge: Author.

Page 5: Avebury aerial: Pete Glastonbury. Avebury ditch: Peter Lorimer. Stone-206, South perimeter, Cove Stone: Author.

Page 6: Silbury Hill top & bottom: Author. Middle aerial: Pete Glastonbury.

Page 7: WKLB aerial: Pete Glastonbury. Rear chamber: Adam Stanford. Blocking stones & entrance corridor: Author.

Page 8: Cursus aerial: Pete Glastonbury. Antler pick: Adam Stanford. Cursus terminal ditch: Richard Hayward.

Page 9: Durrington Aerial: Pete Glastonbury. South Circle: Peter Dunn. Rat's skull & MPP: Adam Stanford.

Page 10: Peter Dunn.

Page 11: LiDAR map composite: Wessex Archaeology.

Page 14: Upper Left / Upper Right / Bottom Right: Pete Glastonbury. Middle two: Author. Bottom Left: Adam Stanford.

Page 15: Upper Two: Public Domain. Avenue: Adam Stanford. AH-7: Mike Pitts. Hole-97: Arthur Simon.

Page 22: Lower Left: 1960 Postcard. Lower Right: Heywood Sumner, 1926.

Page 26: Top 2: Author. East Trilithon: Simon Banton.

Pages 27: All: Pete Glastonbury.

Page 31: Stones -23, -10, & -16: Simon Banton. Parchmarks: Tim Daw. Stone-11: Author.

Page 32: Stone-3, Stones -21, -22, -23: Simon Banton. Entrance & Stone-28 cluster: Author.

Page 33: Stones -12 & -14: Simon Banton. 'Heel' impression: Author.

Page 35: Peter Dunn / English Heritage.

Page 36: Sammy Glastonbury, BS-42, -68, -62 & 63: Pete Glastonbury. Bluestones -66 & -36: Public Domain.

Page 37: All: Simon Banton.

Page 38: Lintel diagram: Peter Dunn / English Heritage. Lintel-160: Simon Banton. Lintel-156: Unknown. Two others: Author.

Page 40: Avenue illustration: Peter Lorimer. Two Avenue aerials: Pete Glastonbury. Avenue ground shot: Author.

Page 41: Adam Stanford.

Page 42: Winter Solstice Sunset: Peter Dunn. 2015 Summer Solstice Sunrise: The BBC.

Page 43: All six: Author.

Page 49: All Unknown.

Page 51: Sumerian tablet: Wikipedia. The Bush Barrow Lozenge: Author.

Page 53: Aerial: Pete Glastonbury. 1906 Sharpe aerial: Public Domain.

Page 55: Skeleton Top: Wessex Archaeology. Skeleton Bottom: Wiltshire Museum, Devizes.

Page 57: L-156 1: Unknown. L-156 2: Tim Daw. Axes on Stone-54: Pete Glastonbury. Axes on Stone-4: Wessex Archaeology. Stone-21 breakage: Author.

Page 59: Top Left: John Jenkins Cole. Top Right: William Judd. Middle: William Hawley / Public Domain. Bottom Two: Richard Atkinson / Public Domain.

Page 60: Pete Glastonbury: Six. Bluestone-150: Dan Rendell.

Page 61: Samantha & Pete Glastonbury: Todd Howard. All others: Pete Glastonbury.

Page 62: Pete Glastonbury.

Page 65: Pete Glastonbury.

Page 66: All eight: Public Domain.

Author Photo: Simon Banton, Nikon D-3.

●

All efforts have been made to obtain identity, permission, or rights for photos marked *Unknown*. If anyone finds the use of their solely owned image objectionable, contact me at: NDWiseman1@gmail.com

All renderings in this book are mine and were created using APS CS-4. Some are 45 layers deep. These pictures took an enormous amount of time to research and produce and are accurate to about 12-inches in scale.

FURTHER READING

Stonehenge has always been popular. But unlike so many other ancient sites it is not tucked away, being stuck in full view out there on the Salisbury Plain. So, looming large in the collective conscience, there have been over 600 books written on the subject in the last 300 years, some concise, many whimsical and several that are just downright goofy. They cannot all be tallied here of course, but a few of the more influential are listed below. Because no one volume can fully encompass the monument, with all its mysteries and many theories, I recommend exploring each of them.

Stonehenge in its Landscape.
Cleal, Walker, and Montague

Stonehenge Complete
Christopher Chippendale

Stonehenge:
Making Sense of a Prehistoric Mystery
Mike Parker Pearson, *et al*

Stonehenge — A History in Photographs
Julian Richards

Stonehenge: Solving the Neolithic Universe
Jonathan M Morris

Hengeworld
Mike Pitts

Stonehenge
John North

Stonehenge Decoded
Gerald S. Hawkins and John B. White

Stonehenge: The Secret of the Solstice
Terence Meaden and George Terence Meaden

Stonehenge — Today and Yesterday
Frank Stevens

A Brief History of Stonehenge
Aubrey Burl

Stonehenge: Plans, Description, And Theories
Sir William Matthew Flinders Petrie

On Stonehenge
Sir Fred Hoyle

Exploring Avebury:
The Essential Guide
Steve Marshall

Stonehenge and Avebury:
Exploring the World Heritage Site
English Heritage

ND Wiseman   Winter Solstice 2017

ABOUT THE AUTHOR

ND Wiseman is a 60-something social observer who has written extensively on a few untidy historical and cultural mysteries which required a more objective analysis, such as Vikings in North America, debunking the fake Moon Landing nonsense, the Titanic, the JFK assassination, and now, his greatest passion, Stonehenge and the Neolithic Era.

He has also written two prehistoric fantasy/adventure novels, one of which is actually pretty good.

Now a hard-bitten, garrulous eccentric, he can be found wrapped in a tattered shawl, huddled over a keyboard in the ramshackle garret of an undisclosed Cape Cod, Massachusetts location while writing about himself in the third-person.

www.ingramcontent.com/pod-product-compliance
Lightning Source LLC
Chambersburg PA
CBHW061054090426
42742CB00002B/43